Listening

Andrew D. Wolvin
University of Maryland, College Park

Carolyn Gwynn Coakley

D1432406

wcb
Wm. C. Brown Company Publishers
Dubuque, Iowa

Copyright © 1982 Wm. C. Brown Company Publishers

Library of Congress Catalog Card Number: 81-66717

ISBN 0-697-04192-1

Second Printing, 1982

Printed in the United States of America

Listening

contents

preface

This basic text is intended for those who want to understand the nature of listening in the process of human communication. It is designed for students who wish to understand (and improve) their own behaviors as receivers in many dimensions.

As communication scholars and educators focus on interpersonal communication and reading behaviors of students, the responsibilities of the receiver as an equal partner in the communication process becomes clear. Yet most of the literature and research in this field stress the source and skip past the role of listener. Analysis of communication time supports the idea that most people spend more time listening than speaking, reading, and writing. Thus, listening is significant.

Interest in listening is found in college and university courses, in units in basic speech communication courses, and in a wide variety of programs developing in language arts and reading in elementary and secondary schools. Many corporate and industrial organizations have added listening training to their programs for employees.

Communication scholars recognize the difficulty in identifying precisely what is involved in the skills of listening behavior.[1] Much of this difficulty lies in the problem of testing these skills. An emphasis on comprehension in such tests makes one wonder if we are determining *listening* skills, or testing *thinking* (and memory) skills.

While it is difficult to pinpoint precisely the difference between listening and thinking, instruction in listening skills can yield benefits. We once assumed that knowing how to organize a speech would enable a person to prepare and present a speech and to listen comprehensively to the speeches of others. Such an assumption about transferring skills may be hasty. Students testify that learning about listening skills in their academic lives is useful in undoing old habits and replacing them with improved listening practices.

The principles in this book are drawn from the research in the field of listening behavior as well as from a variety of disciplines: speech communication, reading, psychology, education, and sociology. The research provides the foundation for the theoretical and for the practical aspects which are incorporated into the book.

This book is designed to provide students with a foundation in the theory and research on the process of listening as the basis for knowing about listening behavior and, then, applying that knowledge to their own skills development. To that end, we have begun with a view of listening as a *communication* skill within the context of the entire human communication process. The reader is introduced to the specific functions within our understanding of listening behavior. These chapters are followed with chapters which treat different listening purposes—appreciative, discriminative, comprehensive, therapeutic, and critical. These chapters are designed to provide readers with an understanding about their listening responses to these different objectives and, further, with some ideas as to enhancing their own skills within these areas.

While an understanding about listening is critical to improving one's own listening behavior, we also think it is useful to know about the primary role of listening in human communication (as treated in our first chapter) and to reflect on individual listening skills as we respond in different settings. To that end, we have developed Chapter 9 to treat listening in such dimensions as conversation, interviewing, public speaking, etc. And we feel strongly that the listener not only must know about listening and attempt to improve skills as a listener, but also must meet certain obligations or responsibilities as a communicator. Since the listener must share at least 50% of the responsibility for effective communication, it is helpful to look at that responsibility in Chapter 10.

Through listening, we can grow as individuals and in our relationships with others.

Notes

1. For a review of this issue, see Robert N. Bostrom and Carol L. Bryant, "Factors in the Retention of Information Presented Orally: The Role of Short-term Listening," *Western Journal of Speech Communication,* 44 (Spring, 1980): 137–145.

acknowledgments

Putting together a book requires the support and assistance of many people. We are especially appreciative to Jim Coakley and Darlyn Wolvin for their patience, understanding, and empathetic listening through the process. We are grateful to Brad and Brooke Wolvin, five-year-old twins pictured on page 64, who consistently demonstrate that skills in good listening *can* be developed at an early age. And we continue to be indebted to our listening students at High Point Senior High School, the University of Maryland at College Park and at University College, and at the U.S. Department of State Foreign Service Institute. Their ideas, interests, and responses have helped to shape our ideas about listening and have given us the framework for these ideas. We also appreciate the support and encouragement we have received from our colleagues in the newly formed International Listening Association. Interaction in this professional association provides us with an exciting forum of listening scholars, teachers, and practitioners.

Readers familiar with our earlier publication, *Listening Instruction* by the ERIC Clearinghouse on Reading and Communication Skills, will recognize some of our ideas about the process of listening. We appreciate the support of William Work, Director of the ERIC Speech Communication Association Module, in our development of this text.

Additionally, we are grateful to our photographer, Bob Tocha, and our illustrator, Ted Metzger, president of Visual Technics, Inc. Both willingly shared their time and creativity with us.

No book can "happen" without the tremendous editorial support we have received from William C. Brown Company Publishers. Our editor, Louise Waller, and our reviewers, Linda Heun of Northeast Missouri State University, Ralph Nichols, Professor Emeritus of the University of Minnesota, and Sally Haug of the University of Wisconsin at Eau Claire, certainly have played a major role in putting this book in final form.

Finally, we want to thank you, our readers, for your interest in listening and for your dedication to improving your own listening skills. We think listening should be a major communication objective for everyone.

concepts you will encounter

Hearing without Listening
Tuning Out
Listening with Understanding
Basic Language Skill
Verbal Communication Time
Listening's Role
Mass Media Demands
Listening's Influence
Two-Step Flow of Communication
Listening Instruction
Costliness of Poor Listening

the need for effective listening

"Is anyone *really* listening?" is a question that is too frequently asked in an age when so much of our communicating is done orally. Unfortunately, many people fail to realize that *meaningful* oral communication is a result of *both* the sending *and* the receiving of messages. If only our ears were as actively involved as our mouths, our failure to listen would not be such a vital concern to so many individuals.

Our Failure to Listen

Daily, individuals—ranging from singers and cartoonists to business executives and counselors—are calling attention to our failure to listen. Let us examine what some of these individuals are saying about this problem that is so prevalent in our society.

In the song, "The Sounds of Silence," Paul Simon has written

And in the naked light I saw
Ten thousand people, maybe more—
People talking without speaking,
People hearing without listening. . . .[1]

Who is hearing without listening? Nation to nation? The young to the old? The old to the young? Child to parent? Parent to child? Employer to employee? Employee to employer? Husband to wife? Wife to husband? We cannot say that these people are not listening to each other because they do not agree with one another on various issues, for listening does not mean agreeing.[2] Listening does mean engaging in three separate but interrelated steps included in the listening process: hearing and attending to the speaker and making an honest effort to understand what the speaker is saying.

Too frequently, we do not engage in the total listening process; instead, we mechanically or mentally tune out the speaker. The practice of mechanically tuning out the speaker can be seen in the person who, opposing all "handouts," changes the television channel when a welfare agent begins to speak. A much more common practice—mentally tuning out the speaker or "closing our ear-lids"—is illustrated in this cartoon caption: A husband, looking at his wife, says

"Go ahead. Keep talking, Martha; I've tuned you out."[3] Mentally tuning out the speaker also is demonstrated in the following human interest article:

> Communication . . . requires . . . listening carefully and trying to understand the message of others.
> We need to do less talking and more listening.
> One schoolboy said to another, "My teacher talks to herself."
> His friend replied, "That's nothing. So does our principal, but he doesn't know it. He thinks everybody's listening."[4]

Unfortunately, many listening scholars believe that our failure to listen too often stems from a lack of "model" listening behavior from those whom we tend to imitate. If those in the positions to be role models—for example, parents and teachers—do not demonstrate effective listening behavior, it is unlikely that children and students will develop effective listening behavior. The following impressive public service announcement illustrates a type of listening behavior that far too many children encounter:

> A father is reading a newspaper when his son enters the room and says, "Hey, Pop? Can I talk to you?"
> The father, never looking up from the paper, says, "Sure, what is it?"
> First, the son discusses school; he says, "I'm gonna be short some credits for graduation, and I'm going to need to go to summer school."
> Dad, who is obviously not listening, responds by saying, "That's good."

The son then makes a second attempt to gain his father's attention. He says, "You know, I think I'll drop out of school, Pop. I'm not going anywhere."

Dad, still reading his paper, mutters, "Well, whattaya know?"

Finally, the son says, "Say, I took my first trip today. That acid. Man, was it groovy."

Dad replies, "Okay. Whatever you think's best."

The son leaves, and the mother enters the room. She asks what the son had said. Dad replies, "Oh, it wasn't important."[5]

But, it was important—important to the son, who did not want his father to be one of those people who hear but do not listen.

Executives of major corporations are also recognizing our failure to listen. They are realizing that inefficient listening is costly—costly in wasted money, misused time, defeated morale, reduced productivity, and alienated relationships. One leading corporation, Sperry, has called attention to its employees' need as well as the public's need to listen by embarking on the corporate theme, "We understand how important it is to listen."[6]

For years, psychotherapists, religious leaders, and counselors have emphasized that many of our relationships deteriorate because we do not listen. Rogers, a psychotherapist, believes that the major barrier to communication is our tendency to react to a statement by forming an evaluation of it from our own point of view. Rogers believes that this barrier can be avoided if we listen to one another with understanding. Listening with understanding requires that the listener make a sincere attempt "to see the expressed idea and attitude from the other person's point of view, to sense how it feels to him, to achieve his frame of reference in regard to the thing he is talking about."[7] The need to listen with understanding is also being communicated by the clergy and by counselors. In the midst of a wedding ceremony we attended, the priest advised the young couple always to keep the channels of communication open, always to listen to one another, and never to build a wall between them. He further stressed that marriage counselors have found that the inability to listen ranks high on the list of qualities that make a marriage fail.[8]

The examples and individuals we have cited have stressed that people frequently do not listen. Do people not listen because listening is unimportant in our society? Because listening proficiency is insignificant in our language development? Because we devote little time to listening in our daily lives? Because the role of listening in our lives is minor? Because listening has little effect or influence on us? Because listening as a skill has not received instructional emphasis in the schools? Let us look at these possibilities.

The Importance of Listening

How important is listening in contemporary society? How do we assess the importance of listening? One way is to examine the position that listening has in our language development. A second way is to determine the amount of time we devote to listening every day. Another way is to explore the role of listening in our lives. Still another way is to discover the effects or influence that listening has on us. These criteria will be used as we investigate the importance of listening.

Listening's Position in Our Language Development

Of the four major areas of language development, listening is the most basic. Listening is the first language skill that we develop; as children, we listen before we speak, speak before we read, and read before we write.[9] Thus, our ability to speak, read, and write is directly and indirectly dependent upon our ability to listen. If we are not proficient in any one of these skills, we are handicapped in the processes of learning and communicating, two activities that are necessary for us to participate productively in modern life.

Listening's Demands on Our Time

Throughout all levels of our educational development, listening is the main channel of classroom instruction. This can be seen readily from "Show and Tell" periods at the kindergarten level to two-hour lecture sessions at the graduate level. This also can be evidenced by the amount of time students are expected to listen in the classroom. Wilt found that elementary students are supposed to listen 57.5 percent of their classroom activity time. She also found that, of the children's time spent in listening, 54 percent is spent listening to the teacher.[10] Markgraf found that high school students are expected to spend 46 percent of their classroom time listening, and that 66 percent of this listening time is spent listening to the teacher.[11] At the college level, Bird discovered that college women spend 42 percent of their daily communication time listening. He also found that 82 percent of his subjects considered listening to be equal to or more important than reading as a factor contributing to academic success in college.[12] The results of these studies demonstrate that listening is a major vehicle for learning in the classroom.

The importance of listening in learning and communicating is also apparent in our daily lives. Not only do we spend more time listening than we spend in any other form of verbal communication, but also, thanks to modern technological advancements, we engage in considerable interpersonal communication and mass communication.

In a landmark study dating back to 1926, Rankin—investigating the frequency of use of listening in the ordinary lives of adults—found that listening is the most frequently used form of verbal communication. Adults spend 29.5 percent of their waking hours listening and 42.1 percent of their total verbal communication time listening, while they spend 31.9 percent, 15 percent, and 11 percent of their verbal communication time speaking, reading, and writing.[13] Three more recent investigations have supported Rankin's finding that listening is the most important form of verbal communication in daily life. In 1957 Brieter investigated the frequency of use of listening in the lives of housewives; she found that they spend 48 percent of their verbal communication time listening (followed by speaking, reading, and writing—in that order).[14] In 1974 Weinrauch and Swanda expanded on Rankin's study; they investigated the amount of time that 46 business personnel (including those with top, middle, and lower managerial responsibilities and those with no managerial responsibilities) spend in direct communication (reading, writing, speaking, and listening) during a typical work week. They found that the business participants spend 32.7 percent of their total direct verbal communication time listening, 25.8 percent speaking, 22.6 percent writing, and 18.8 percent reading. Although the percentage of time spent listening is lower in this study than it is in the other cited studies, it must be noted that this study does not include the amount of time the business participants spend listening beyond their working hours.[15] In 1975, Werner conducted an update study of the 1926 Rankin study. Utilizing 166 subjects (including high school and college students, housewives, and employees in a variety of occupations), she found that they spend 54.93 percent of their verbal communication time listening while they spend 23.19 percent, 13.27 percent, and 8.40 percent of their verbal communication time speaking, reading, and writing.[16] Studies investigating the frequency of use of listening in and out of the classroom reveal that listening consumes more of our daily communication time than does any other form of verbal communication; hence, quantitatively, listening is the most important form of verbal communication.

Listening's Role in Our Lives

Because modern technological advancements have enabled us to gather together as groups with greater ease, the role of listening in interpersonal, as well as group and public, communicative situations has become more significant in the mental, economic, spiritual, political, and social aspects of our lives. Whether the purpose of our assemblage is to settle differences between nations (such as the talks between the Iranians and the Americans), to investigate a country's affairs (such as the Senate Watergate Hearings), to advance a common cause (such as speakouts regarding the passage of the Equal Rights Amendment), or to search for or strengthen social ties (such as singles' parties and block parties), listening plays a vital role in our attempts to achieve our goals.

The importance of listening has also been accented by advancements in the mass media. With the arrival of radio, motion pictures, and television, we have come to rely more and more on the spoken word for information about local, state, national, and international affairs as well as for enjoyment. The mass media advancements, as well as the quickened pace of life, have aided in creating a shift from the eye and the printed page to the ear and the word of mouth. The demands that the mass media presently make on our ears appear to be only in the initial stages; the predictions of what is to come in the mass communications field indicate that listening will occupy an increasing amount of our time in the future.

The increasing importance of the spoken word—in this mass communications revolution—can be gauged by the number of radio and television sets in American homes and the amount of time these sets are in operation. Data compiled by the A.C. Nielson Company in 1955 revealed that 97 percent of American households owned one or more radios and that the radio was in use two hours and twenty-seven minutes per day (as calculated by audio-meters installed on all radio sets in a nationally selected sample of American homes). The data also revealed that 46.2 million television sets were in use and that the television was on three hours and thirty-nine seconds per day.[17] According to 1980 Arbitron statistics, the average American increased his or her weekly radio listening time by two and a half hours from 1955 to 1980.[18] Nielson's 1979 report shows a considerable increase in both of the previously reported estimates regarding television ownership and use; as of September 1, 1978 an estimated 74.5 million households (or 98 percent of all households in the United States) owned at least one television set, and during the 1977–78 television season the average television household viewed an estimated six hours and thirteen minutes of television per day.[19] In a survey of televiewing in the Chicago area in 1960, Witty found that elementary children, high school students, parents, and teachers spend 21 hours, 14 hours, 20 hours, and 12 hours, respectively, per week listening to and viewing television.[20] According to the 1979 Nielson report, the estimated weekly viewing time of different American age groups in February 1978, was as follows:

Women ages 55 and over	37 hours and 55 minutes
Women ages 25 to 54	33 hours and 54 minutes
Men ages 55 and over	33 hours and 38 minutes
Women ages 18 to 24	32 hours and 53 minutes
Children ages 2 to 5	31 hours and 23 minutes
Children ages 6 to 11	27 hours and 16 minutes
Male teens	27 hours and 12 minutes
Men ages 25 to 54	26 hours and 42 minutes
Men ages 18 to 24	23 hours and 32 minutes
Female teens	23 hours and 25 minutes[21]

Lundsteen estimates (and her estimate is supported by the 1979 Nielson report) that young people—from ages 3 to 18—spend some 22 thousand hours before television sets.[22]

Listening's Influence on Our Personal Development

Recognizing that listening is the most basic skill in our language development, that listening is the most frequently used form of verbal communication, and that listening plays a significant role in our daily lives (both in and out of the classroom), we then—in assessing the importance of listening—attempt to discover the effect or influence that listening has on our personal development. The Commission on the English Curriculum of the National Council of Teachers of English believes that people's "economic concepts, political ideals, and ethical standards are influenced, if not largely determined, by their listening."[23] Since much of our listening time is spent listening to the media, we should examine how the media affects us. According to McLuhan and Fiore, the electric media "far surpasses any possible influence mom and dad can now bring to bear. . . . Now all the world's a stage."[24] They further stress the impact that the media has on us:

> All media work us over completely. They are so persuasive in their personal, political, economic, aesthetic, psychological, moral, ethical, and social consequences that they leave no part of us untouched, unaffected, unaltered. The medium is the massage.[25]

The Commission on the English Curriculum also recognizes the impact that the media has on us; the commission has emphasized that many of our attitudes, principles, understandings, and ideas are being increasingly "left to the tutelage of the radio, talking pictures, and television."[26]

Additional sources have noted the impact that one particular medium—television—has on us. Testifying before the Commission on Violence, Gerbner commented on the influence of television:

> In only two decades of massive national existence television has transformed the political life of a nation, has changed the daily habits of our people, has moulded the style of the generation, . . . redirected the flow of information and values from traditional channels into centralized networks reaching into every home . . . it has profoundly affected what we call the process of socialization, the process by which members of our species become human.[27]

Further emphasizing the effects of television, the Interim Report of the Dodd Committee in 1965 concluded "that television, whose impact on the public mind is equal to or greater than that of any other medium, is a factor in molding the character, attitudes, and behavior patterns of America's young people. . . ."[28] According to Charles D. Ferris, chairman of the Federal Communication Commission, "television has influenced our national and international affairs—from civil rights, Vietnam, and Watergate to Afghanistan and Iran. . . . It makes viewers participants in these events, and viewer reactions add another dimension to the events themselves."[29]

Although studies of the mass media have demonstrated that the spoken word is influential in the formation of habits and attitudes, they have also revealed that the mass media does not have as much of a direct influence on us as our interpersonal contacts do.[30] Results of several experimental studies have led Katz to hypothesize that any effect of the mass media on the general public normally operates through a "two-step flow of communication"; that is, ideas flow from the mass media to "opinion leaders" (friends, co-workers, family members, or any "significant others") and from them to the rest of the community. Thus, personal contact serves to influence us more than the mass media (although many of the ideas we discuss with others originate from the mass media).[31] This hypothesis does not lessen the importance of listening as an influential force in our lives, however, for listening is as much a part of interpersonal communication as it is a part of mass communication.

Let us now summarize how important listening is in contemporary society. It is the most basic skill in our language development; it is the most frequently used language skill; it plays an integral part in our everyday lives; and it appears to have a profound effect on the formation of our attitudes, skills, behavioral patterns, and understandings. The importance of listening has received ample endorsement:

> Listening can make the difference between knowledge and ignorance, information and misinformation, involvement and detachment, enjoyment and boredom.[32]

> The art of listening holds for us the desperate hope of withstanding the spreading ravages of commercial, nationalistic, and ideological persuasion.[33]

> What this country needs is not a good five-cent cigar. What this country needs is more good listeners![34]

The Schools' Instructional Emphasis on Listening

In spite of the importance of listening, instructional emphasis on the development of adequate listening ability in American schools has been slight. Although an accepted principle of curriculum making is that students "ought to be taught to do well those things which current living demands of them,"[35] America's educational system has, quantitatively, nearly placed an inverted interest on the four major language art skills.

In 1929, Rankin found that the schools' instructional emphasis on reading and writing was 52 percent and 30 percent respectively, while the schools' instructional emphasis on speaking and listening was 10 percent and 8 percent respectively.[36] Still today, the two oral language arts skills are receiving less instructional attention. This neglect of the schools has been recognized by the Speech Communication Association (formerly known as the Speech Association of America): "For years the skills of oral communication have been neglected, or have been taught only incidentally or sporadically in most of our elementary and secondary schools."[37]

The most neglected language art skill at all educational levels, however, is listening. As we reflect upon our own early school days, how many of us can recall any structured listening training? Most of us can remember the numerous times that we, as "Blue Birds" (or, depending on our reading readiness, the "Red Birds" or "Yellow Birds"), were called to the reading circle where we became more and more proficient at reading about the activities of Jim, Judy, Tags, and Twinkle (or of people and animals with other names). Most of us can also remember the many hours that we—being closely watched by our teachers—sat at our desks and practiced drawing ovals and straight (very straight) lines on that wide-spaced yellow paper; we remember practicing and practicing until we had mastered printing, and, then, we began practicing many more hours until we had perfected cursive writing. Many of us, too, may remember the many times our teachers corrected our incorrect word choice and grammatical errors and our own special moments in front of the class when we showed and told. Can any of us, though, remember receiving structured, meaningful listening training? Too frequently, the only "instruction" in listening that we received was requests and commands to pay attention and/or a few lists of listening dos and don'ts. As we reflect upon our later school days (from junior high through higher education), we recall that we continued to receive little or no training in developing our proficiency in listening—the "skill" we most frequently use.

The fact that listening still remains the "orphan" of the language arts can be easily affirmed by the reports of several listening scholars who have investigated the status of the teaching of listening. In 1948, only one school in America—Stephens College—was teaching listening. Anderson, having corresponded with hundreds of teachers throughout the country, found that listening was being taught in very few schools in 1952.[38] Five years later, Letton reported that evidence demonstrating that listening was being taught in the schools was scarce.[39] In 1962, Brown and Keller noted that, although there were approximately 50 thousand speech courses taught in institutions of higher learning, there was "only a handful of courses in listening." They believed that these findings demonstrate that Americans "have conceived the dual act of speaking and listening almost entirely from the speaker's point of view."[40] The almost exclusive focus on the transmission of messages has contributed to the neglect of the receptive aspect of the oral communication process. Markgraf—having surveyed 406 teacher-training institutions in 1962—reported that only three institutions offered specialized courses in listening and that 134 institutions taught listening as a separate unit.[41]

These findings indicate that the schools have been negligent in providing instruction in listening, the basic language skill. Apparently, many educators have not realized what the omission of listening in the language arts instructional program means as much as one sixth-grade girl has. After listening to Brown speak of the importance of auding (listening), she inquired, "Then leaving out auding in language would be like leaving out home plate in baseball, huh?"[42] A portion of one of Sperry's advertisements summarizes the schools' emphasis on listening: ". . . listening is the one communication skill we're never really taught. We're taught how to read, to write, to speak—but not to listen."[43]

Why has instruction in listening received such slight emphasis in the American schools? Scholars in the field have suggested many reasons why the teaching of listening has been neglected. Anderson has suggested two possible reasons: the first is that the eye still holds dominance over the ear to many school administrators and teachers who received their education in a day when the spoken word was of relatively less importance, and, thus, many educators fail to acknowledge the importance of listening now; and the second is that deficiencies in listening are not easily detected.[44] Nichols reported that nonprofessionals attributed the neglect to their belief that "listening is probably determined by hearing acuity and intelligence, and that the schools can do comparatively little about either one" and that university staff members felt that the neglect was probably due to the "widespread assumption that *practice* and intelligence are the only significant components of efficient listening."[45] Still another reason might be that the school curriculum is already overcrowded.

Spearritt, as well as other listening scholars, has advanced the argument that listening has received so little attention because of the assumption that growth in listening skills is automatic and, therefore, instruction is unnecessary.[46] Since many children who come to first grade appear to have acquired—without systematic training—relatively adequate oral communication skills, many educators assume that, through normal classroom activities at the various educational levels, students will develop listening skills sufficient to meet their needs.

Does experimental evidence support this assumption? Although they were measuring students' listening habits (rather than their capacity to listen), Nichols and Stevens conducted a study in which they investigated the percentage of students who could tell what their teachers were talking about when the teachers stopped in the middle of their lectures. The investigators found that 90 percent of the first graders, 80 percent of the second graders, 43.7 percent of the junior high students, and 28 percent of the senior high students could correctly answer the question.[47] Studies by Jones and Nichols, among others, have revealed that, without direct listening training, college subjects correctly answer 50 percent of the items on an immediate recall test (covering the material in a ten-minute lecture) and 25 percent of the items on a delayed recall test.[48]

Lundsteen has speculated that the schools' neglect of the teaching of listening may be due to the fact that teachers have had little, if any, listening training and/or instruction in methods in teaching listening.[49] When Markgraf surveyed 406 teacher-training institutions in 1962, he found that less than half of the institutions (44 percent) included units on methods of teaching listening in their methods courses.[50]

Still another reason why listening training has been neglected in the schools may be that there is a scarcity of instructional materials pertaining to listening. The findings of Heilman, Lynch and Evans, and Brown demonstrate that most instructional materials are sparse and lacking in substance. Heilman examined textbooks on teaching and curriculum guides to ascertain their treatment, if any, of listening. He found that 11 out of 15 textbooks published between 1946 and 1954 did not mention listening. Heilman also found that, although many curriculum guides appeared to respect the role of listening in the educational process, they included few concrete suggestions for developing skill in listening.[51] In 1963, Lynch and Evans analyzed the content of 14 series of high school English textbooks to discover the number of pages devoted to listening. They found that, of a total of 26,141 pages, 424 were concerned with listening.[52] In 1967, Brown analyzed the content of 54 language arts textbooks (published between 1959 and

1964) for grades 3 through 6. He found that listening was emphasized in only .63 percent of the lessons and on .57 percent of the pages.[53] The presence or absence of listening material in textbooks and curriculum guides does not necessarily indicate the presence or absence of listening instruction in the classroom; however, it seems reasonable to assume that teachers do utilize textbooks and courses of study as guides for what subject matter will be covered in the classroom. The fact that the first full-length book on listening, *Are You Listening?*, was not published until 1957 further emphasizes the lag that exists in the area of listening.[54]

Not until 1978 did the federal government join those who believe that listening should be taught. In the 1978 Primary and Secondary Education Act, the government added listening and speaking—to reading, writing, and arithmetic—as measures of literacy and as needed basic competencies. Perhaps this legislation will prove to be the impetus that the educational system needs to stop neglecting the teaching of the basic communication skill—listening.

The Business World's Reaction to Ineffective Listening

As a result of the educational lag in developing the listening efficiency of students, many leading corporations are recognizing that untrained listeners who were once students are now employees and that inefficient listening in business is costly. Lyman K. Steil, president of Communication Development, Inc., and a professor of listening at the University of Minnesota, estimates that poor listening costs American businesses billions of dollars:

> With more than 100 million workers in this country, a simple $10 mistake by each of them, as a result of poor listening, would add up to a cost of a billion dollars. And most people make numerous listening mistakes every week.
>
> Because of listening mistakes, letters have to be retyped, appointments rescheduled, shipments rerouted. Productivity is affected and profits suffer.[55]

Many executives are not only becoming more aware of but also believing more in Nichols's findings that the average white-collar worker demonstrates only about 25 percent listening efficiency.[56] They also are beginning to agree with the view that one of the greatest and most common weaknesses of most marketers, especially those in selling, is the failure to recognize that listening is equal in importance to talking.[57] Furthermore, they are beginning to adopt the following view:

> The most important factor for successful communication is not only the ability to use language well or to speak well or to present one's own point of view; it is rather the ability to listen well to the other person's point of view.[58]

Finally, they are beginning to perceive listening as, in the words of Keefe, "the key not only to getting the job done but to peaceful growth and economic success as well."[59]

Recognizing the costliness of poor listening and the importance of effective listening from the executive suite to the shop floor, executives in many leading corporations are providing listening training for their employees. Among those corporations that are currently including listening training in their formal training programs are Sperry, Xerox, Pfizer, 3M, American Telephone and Telegraph, General Electric, Dun and Bradstreet, Pitney Bowes, Stamford, and CT. These companies are doing more than acknowledging the importance of effective listening; they are working toward eliminating the question, "Is anyone *really* listening?"

Summary

In this chapter, we have called attention to the costly communication barriers that often result when we do not engage in the total listening process—the process of hearing, attending to, and understanding the sender's message. Also, we have shown that listening is the most basic of the four major areas of language development; that listening is the most frequently used form of verbal communication and, thus, plays a significant role in our educational, personal, and professional lives; and that listening appears to have a profound effect on the formations of our attitudes, skills, behaviors, and understandings. Lastly, we have stressed that, in spite of the importance of listening, America's schools—at all educational levels—have been negligent in providing instruction in listening due to numerous reasons ranging from the failure of educators to recognize the importance of listening to the scarcity of instructional material pertaining to listening. As a result of the schools' slight enphasis on the development of adequate listening skills, many leading corporations are recognizing the need to provide listening training for their employees so that costly communication barriers resulting from poor listening will be minimized or completely eliminated.

Activities to Try

1. Collect articles, cartoons, lines from songs and commercials, quotes, etc., that call attention to ineffective listening, and then orally share them with the class.
2. Compile a list of listening skills that you need to improve or develop in order for you to be an effective listener in your *personal* life. Orally share this list with the class.
3. Maintain a listening log for a period of a week. Construct daily time charts divided into fifteen-minute intervals. Using S (for speaking), W (for writing), R (for reading), L (for listening), and N (for nonverbal communication or no communication), code your communication time during each waking hour. Use the code that represents the type of communication in which you

engage the *majority* of each fifteen-minute interval. Then tabulate the following:

a. The total number of fifteen-minute intervals you were awake.
b. The total number of fifteen-minute intervals you engaged in no (or nonverbal) communication.
c. The total number of fifteen-minute intervals you engaged in *each* type of verbal communication: speaking, writing, reading, and listening.
d. The total number of fifteen-minute intervals you engaged in verbal communication (a sum of the four totals calculated in c).
e. The percentage of waking hours you spent engaged in no (or nonverbal) communication, verbal communication, writing, reading, listening, and speaking.

Finally, compare your findings with Rankin's findings, which are as follows:

No (or nonverbal) communication	30 percent
Verbal communication	70 percent
Listening	42.1 percent
Speaking	31.9 percent
Reading	15 percent
Writing	11 percent[60]

4. From your listening logs, determine the percentage of time you are expected to listen in your classes.
5. From your listening logs, determine the percentage of time you are expected to listen on your jobs. Then, compare your findings with those of Weinrauch and Swanda.
6. Maintain a seven-day listening log of time you spend listening to television. Then, calculate the average number of hours you listen to television per day and compare your personal television viewing habits with those reported in the *1979 Nielson Report on Television.*
7. Explore the importance of good listening in your planned or chosen profession/vocation. Interview, in person or over the telephone, at least one person working in your field of interest. Among the questions you should ask are the following:

Specifically, what is your occupation?

During a typical work day, what percentage of the day do you spend in verbally communicating with others?

Rank the four means of verbal communication in which you engage (reading, writing, listening, and speaking) from the one you use most to the one you use the least.

List specific situations in which you engage in listening.

In your area of specialization, how important is listening?

What specific listening skills does a person holding your position need to possess?

Do you consider yourself a good listener? Why or why not?

Does your company provide any direct listening training? If so, what kind of training?

After conducting the interview(s), discuss your findings on paper.

Submit a copy of your findings to all other students and the instructor.[61]

8. Contact educators at the elementary, secondary, and college levels and investigate what, if any, direct listening instruction they provide and why they do or do not provide it. Then, share your findings with the class.

9. Contact several local companies and find out if any of them provide direct listening training for their employees. If they do, you are to inquire about the type of training that is provided. Then, share your findings with the class.

Notes

1. © 1964, 1965 Paul Simon Used by permission.
2. Carl H. Weaver, *Human Listening: Processes and Behavior* (Bobbs-Merrill Company, 1972), p. 22.
3. *Washington Star,* 19 October 1971, p. A–12. Used with permission of Universal Press.
4. "Communicating: Not Easy Job," *Grit* 5 November 1972, p. 32.
5. Franciscan Communications, Public Service Announcement, WJZ-TV, Summer, 1972. Reprinted by permission of the publisher.
6. Advertisement by Sperry, *The Wall Street Journal* 11 September 1979, p. 11. Reprinted by permission of the Sperry Corporation.
7. Carl R. Rogers and F. J. Roethlisberger, "Barriers and Gateways to Communication," *Harvard Business Review* 30 (July 1952):47.
8. Father Walter Norris, nuptial message presented at the University of Maryland Chapel, University of Maryland, August 11, 1973.
9. Sara W. Lundsteen, *Listening: Its Impact on Reading and the Other Language Arts* (Illinois: NCTE/ERIC, 1971), p. 3.
10. Miriam E. Wilt, "A Study of Teacher Awareness of Listening as a Factor in Elementary Education," *Journal of Educational Research* 43 (April 1950): 631.
11. Bruce Markgraf, "An Observational Study Determining the Amount of Time That Students in the Tenth and Twelfth Grades Are Expected to Listen in the Classroom," in *Listening: Readings,* ed. Sam Duker (New York: Scarecrow Press, 1966), pp. 90–94.
12. Donald E. Bird, "Teaching Listening Comprehension," *Journal of Communication* 3 (November 1953): 127–128.
13. Raul Tory Rankin, "The Measurement of the Ability to Understand Spoken Language" (unpublished Ph.D. dissertation, University of Michigan, 1926), *Dissertation Abstracts* 12 (1952): 847–848.
14. Lila R. Brieter, "Research in Listening and Its Importance to Literature," cited by Larry L. Barker, *Listening Behavior* (Englewood Cliffs, New Jersey: Prentice-Hall, 1971), p. 4.
15. J. Donald Weinrauch and John R. Swanda, Jr., "Examining the Significance of Listening: An Exploratory Study of Contemporary Management," *The Journal of Business Communication* 13 (February 1975): 25–32.
16. Elyse K. Werner, "A Study of Communication Time" (M.A. thesis, University of Maryland—College Park, 1975), p. 26.

17. Richard E. Chapin, *Mass Communications—A Statistical Analysis* (Michigan: Michigan State University Press, 1957), pp. 88–97.
18. Miles Maguire, "Baltimore Radio," *The Evening Sun* 20 May 1980, p. C–1.
19. A. C. Nielson Company, *1979 Nielson Report on Television* (Illinois: A. C. Nielson Company, 1979), pp. 3–6.
20. Paul Witty, "Televiewing by Children and Youth," *Elementary English* 28 (February 1961): 105.
21. A. C. Nielson Company, *1979 Nielson Report on Television*, pp. 8–9.
22. Lundsteen, *Listening: Its Impact on Reading and the Other Language Arts*, p. 5.
23. Commission on the English Curriculum of the National Council of Teachers of English, *The English Language Arts* (New York: Appleton-Century-Crofts, 1952), pp. 329–330.
24. From *The Medium Is the Massage* by Marshall McLuhan and Quentin Fiore. Coordinated by Jerome Agel. Copyright © 1967 by Bantam Books, Inc. Reprinted by permission of the publisher. All rights reserved.
25. *Ibid.*
26. Commission on the English Curriculum of the National Council of Teachers of English, *The English Language Arts*, pp. 329–330.
27. Dean George Gerbner, quoted in Nicholas Johnson, *How to Talk Back to Your TV Set* (Boston: Little, Brown and Company, 1970), p. 24.
28. The Interim Report of the Dodd Committee, quoted in Nicholas Johnson, *How to Talk Back to Your TV Set*, p. 37.
29. Charles D. Ferris, "The FCC Takes a Hard Look at Television," *Today's Education* 69 (September/October 1980): 66GS.
30. Daryl J. Bem, *Beliefs, Attitudes, and Human Affairs* (Belmont, California: Brooks/Cole Publishing Company, 1970), pp. 75–77.
31. Elihu Katz, "The Two-Step Flow of Communication: An Up-to-Date Report on a Hypothesis," *Public Opinion Quarterly* 1 (1957): 61–78.
32. Commission on the English Curriculum of the National Council of Teachers of English, *The English Language Arts in the Secondary School* (New York: Appleton-Century-Croft, 1956), p. 251.
33. Wendell Johnson, "Do We Know How to Listen?" *ETC* 7 (Autumn 1949): 3.
34. Dr. Walt Menninger's column "What We All Need Is a Good Listener" Copyright, 1979, Universal Press Syndicate. All rights reserved.
35. Harold A. Anderson, "Needed Research in Listening," *Elementary English* 29 (April 1954): 216.
36. Paul Tory Rankin, "Listening Ability: Its Improvement, Measurement, and Development," *Chicago Schools Journal* 12 (January, June 1930): 177–179, 417–420.
37. Speech Association of America, "Speech Education in the Public Schools," *Speech Teacher* 16 (January 1967): 79.
38. Anderson, "Needed Research in Listening," 221.
39. Mildred C. Letton, "The Status of the Teaching of Listening," *Elementary School Journal* 57 (January 1957): 181.
40. Charles T. Brown and Paul W. Keller, "A Modest Proposal for Listening Training," *Quarterly Journal of Speech* 48 (December 1962): 395.
41. Bruce Markgraf, "Listening Pedagogy in Teacher-Training Institutions," *Journal of Communication* 12 (March 1962): 34.

42. Donald P. Brown, "What Is the Basic Language Skill?" *ETC* 14 (Winter 1956–1957): 118.

43. Advertisement by Sperry. Reprinted by permission of the Sperry Corporation.

44. Harold Anderson, "Teaching the Art of Listening," *School Review* 57 (February 1949): 66.

45. Ralph G. Nichols, "Listening Instruction in the Secondary School," in *Listening: Readings,* ed. Sam Duker, pp. 242–243.

46. Donald Spearritt, *Listening Comprehension—A Factorial Analysis* (Melbourne, Australia: G. W. and Sons, 1962), p. 3.

47. Ralph G. Nichols and Leonard A. Stevens, *Are You Listening?* (New York: McGraw Hill Book Company, 1957), pp. 12–13.

48. Ralph G. Nichols, "Do We Know How to Listen? Practical Helps in a Modern Age," *Speech Teacher* 10 (March 1961): 119–120.

49. Lundsteen, *Listening: Its Impact on Reading and the Other Language Arts,* p. 8.

50. Markgraf, "Listening Pedagogy in Teacher-Training Institutions," pp. 33–35.

51. Arthur W. Heilman, "Listening and the Curriculum," *Education* 75 (January 1955): 285–286.

52. James J. Lynch and Betrand Evans, *High School English Textbooks: A Critical Examination* (Boston: Little Brown, 1963), pp. 495–496.

53. Kenneth L. Brown, "Speech and Listening in Language Arts Textbooks," *Elementary English* 44 (April 1967): 336–341.

54. Nichols and Stevens, *Are You Listening?*

55. Lyman K. Steil, "Secrets of Being a Better Listener," *U.S. News and World Report* 88 (May 26, 1980): 65.

56. Ralph G. Nichols, "Listening Is a 10-Part Skill," *Nation's Business* 45 (July 1957): 56.

57. Edward W. Wheatley, "Glimpses of Tomorrow," *Sales Management* 104 (May 1, 1970): 41.

58. Weinrauch and Swanda, "Examining the Significance of Listening: An Exploratory Study of Contemporary Management," p. 26.

59. William F. Keefe, *Listen, Management!* (New York: McGraw-Hill Book Company, 1971), p. 192.

60. Andrew D. Wolvin and Carolyn Gwynn Coakley, *Listening Instruction* (Urbana, Illinois: ERIC Clearinghouse on Reading and Communication Skills, 1979), pp. 19–20.

61. *Ibid.,* p. 20.

1

concepts you will encounter

Communication Process
Communication Source
Communication Messages
Communication Channel
Communication Receiver
Communication Feedback
Communication Environment
Communication Noise
Communication Skills
Knowledge
Attitudes
Frame of Reference
Symbolic Language
Transactional Communication

the process of communication

2

As we study listening as a communication behavior, it is useful to view it from the overall perspective of communication as a *process*. Scholars in the communication field have come to recognize the *process* nature of human communication, viewing it as an ongoing, dynamic interaction of components. Communication, as a process, is thus never ending in that one message may well influence yet another and serve as the stimulus for a continuation of the communication.

Components of Communication

As an ongoing human act, then, communication involves a number of components which make up the complex phenomena. There is a communication *source,* a speaker who originates a message. The process begins with an original stimulus (an event, object, person, idea) which the source wishes to communicate. So the source encodes this idea, sorting and selecting symbols in order to translate the idea into a *message* to communicate by way of verbal and nonverbal language symbols.

The encoded message, then, is transcribed via a communication *channel.* In face-to-face communication, the five senses—sight, sound, touch, smell, and taste—serve as the major channels for this transmission. As Americans, we use the auditory and visual channels as our primary media in most communication, while in other cultures touch and smell may be utilized. We also make extensive use of electronic channels in telecommunication (telephone, radio, television) in our society.

The verbal and nonverbal messages, transmitted via these channels, then are received and decoded (filtered and translated into a person's language code in order to assign meaning) by the communication *receiver.* The receiver, in turn, responds to the source, message, and channel by encoding and sending *feedback*— the response/reaction of the receiver as perceived by the source. This feedback creates the ongoing, dynamic nature of the communication process. The source decodes (interprets) the feedback and, ideally, adapts and adjusts the communication accordingly.

Throughout this process, the communication will be affected by two other important components. The *environment*—where the communication takes place—is one of these components. We communicate in specific settings, physical

Figure 2.1.
Simple model of communication.

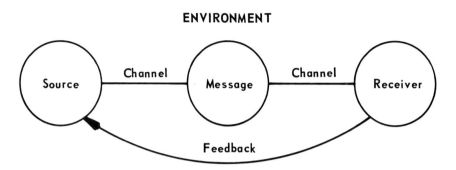

surroundings that will influence us as communicators. Temperatures, ventilation, lighting, room size all affect the outcome of our communication.

We also are affected by *noise*—internal and external interference—throughout the system. This interference can be internal, within the communicators themselves. A word, for example, could throw up an emotional "barrier" and cause the person to lose track of the message being communicated. The interference also can be external to the system—a loud sound in the room, static in the channel, or even a lack of coherency in the message.

The communication components can be depicted in a simple model which illustrates the interaction of the various parts that make up the process:

Communication Variables

Critical to the effectiveness of communication as a human process are variables in the system, factors which facilitate or diminish the outcomes of the communication. We can look at these variables as they affect the different components in the communication process.[1]

One key variable which affects the communication source and receiver is the communication *skill* which the communicators bring to the process. Skills in communication, which are learned by humans from early infancy, include the ability to analyze and adapt to various communicators and communication situations. Abilities in encoding messages might incorporate verbal language facility, skill in structuring messages, and such nonverbal skills as vocal dynamics and physical expressiveness. These elements are important not only to the sending of messages but also to the sending of feedback, responses to messages. Substantial training in speaking and listening skills can aid communicators in their effectiveness with these communication skills.

Communication skills combine with communicator *knowledge* to influence the process of communication. Communicators, both source and receiver, should know about the subject matter under discussion, and they should share information about the verbal and nonverbal language code utilized to convey the messages. Communicators should know about message structure and about environmental control (how to regulate temperature, decrease noise, etc.) in order to communicate more precisely. It is helpful, also, for communicators to know about channel selection—how to choose the most appropriate medium to send a message or to communicate feedback. The more extensive the knowledge about the communication itself, and about the material to be communicated, the more effective the communicators should be.

Likewise, the communicators share *attitudes*—predispositions to respond positively or negatively. These attitudes may be shared toward each other as communicators. A speaker may not care for a group of union representatives he or she must address, for example. Or a listener may be too supportive of a particular political candidate so that he or she overlooks major flaws in the candidate's platform.

These positive and negative attitudes affect us communicators in our orientations toward the message as well. As listeners, we might be so opposed to foreign aid programs, for instance, that we refuse to accept the basic thesis of a message by an official from the Agency for International Development. Or a manager might be asked to brief employees on a new company procedure, a procedure that he or she does not agree is the most efficient method. This attitude, of course, will carry through in his or her presentation of the briefing.

Attitudes can affect us as communicators as well. Considerable research in the communication field indicates that a substantial number of people suffer communication apprehension, anxiety about communicating with others. Speakers who experience "stage fright" may well have negative attitudes toward their own abilities as communicators. And these negative attitudes certainly can influence our self-concepts as listeners. Many people feel they are not effective listeners and, consequently, they are *not* effective listeners. But this negative self-concept may stem from the negative messages we hear as listeners throughout our formative years: "Be quiet and listen"; "You're not listening to me"; "Don't you ever listen?" We seldom hear positive, reinforcing messages about our listening behavior.

Positive and negative attitudes extend to other components of the communication process. We may dislike a particular classroom and, thus, have difficulty paying attention to instruction in the room. Or we may have negative attitudes toward certain communication channels. There are people, for instance, who cannot talk into telephone answering machines. They hang up to avoid the trauma of "At the sound of the tone, please leave your message!"

The attitudes, knowledge, and communication skills of communicators, both speakers and listeners, contribute to the *frame of reference* of the communicators. The frame of reference consists of the background, life experiences, social-cultural context of the individual. All of these elements create the perceptual filter through which we receive stimuli, send messages, and relate to the rest of the world around us. In short, everything that makes up our being as humans becomes part of our communication.

Just as key factors relating to the source and the receiver will affect the outcome of the communication, so, too, will variables of the message itself have an influence on the communication.

The message is composed of the content, structured and presented by way of verbal and nonverbal language code. The content consists of the ideas and the point of view which the communicator wishes to express. Those very ideas may or may not be consistent with the attitudes and the knowledge of the receiver, as we have seen. Consequently, it may be necessary for the source to adjust and adapt the message to more satisfactorily meet the needs of the listener. Norman Thomas, the Socialist candidate for the American Presidency six times, for instance, presented messages in his Socialist platform which were not consistent with basic democratic ideals of most Americans. As a result, Thomas's fundamental messages were never acceptable to the majority of the voters.

The message structure, likewise, influences the understanding of and acceptance of the ideas. Americans, brought up with a Western philosophical orientation, are accustomed to deductive structure, consisting of generalizations leading to a specific conclusion. (Good listeners pay attention to the material. You pay attention to the material. Therefore, you are a good listener.) Persons raised under the influence of Eastern philosophical thought, on the other hand, may not be so accustomed to a deductive structure of messages. While American communicators are trained to develop a message with an introduction, central point, body, and conclusion, Chinese may have a different structure to a message.

KI   (an introduction offering an observation of a concrete reality)
SHO   (tell a story)
TEN   (shift or change in which a new topic or aspect is brought into the message)
KETSU (gathering of loose ends, a "nonconclusion")
YO-IN (a last point to think about which does not necessarily relate)

The audience, then, is allowed to draw its own conclusion; a central point is not presented in such a structure.

The message structure, stemming from the cognitive orientation of the person, extends to the *language code* itself. A key variable in effective communication, the language code (verbal and nonverbal) is central to the entire process.

Important to the comprehension of the verbal message is, of course, the sharing of common language symbols. Through the course of time and through accepted use, we have come to associate certain meanings with words. But the words themselves are empty *representers* of the stimulus we have chosen to communicate.[2] Thus, the word *chair* is a collection of letters arbitrarily assigned to that piece of furniture on which we sit. The word itself represents the chair, much as a road map is used to represent the freeway we travel to work.

Because we use our verbal language to *symbolically* represent that which we intend to communicate, communicators are well advised to remember that it *is* a symbolic process, a process of representing our concepts and objects with words. It is foolish to react to a symbol, a word, as if it were the referent itself. Remembering that it is a symbolic process is particularly important for listeners responding to highly volatile messages—"hate" rhetoric, for instance. We need to set aside our biases and prejudices while decoding communications and remember that speakers are using words to symbolically represent their ideas.

Messages are transmitted not only by symbolic verbal codes but also by nonverbal language—everything but the word itself. Communicators, then, ought to be sensitive to such nonverbal dimensions as vocal inflections and vocal quality; gestures and physical animation; eye contact; and even a person's physical appearance and dress. All of these elements communicate messages about a speaker's emotional state, self-concept, and attitudes toward the communication itself.

The nonverbal and verbal messages are presented via the sensory channels—sound, sight, smell, touch, and taste. Our sensory acuity will greatly influence the effectiveness of these channels. A sensory block can, of course, eliminate the use of a particular channel and perhaps even require persons to compensate through other channels. A deaf or hearing-impaired person, for instance, must make extensive use of visual communication channels in order to lip read, utilize sign language, and "read" the nonverbal cues of the communicator.

The effectiveness of a particular channel at a particular time is influenced not only by the communicator's sensory acuity but also by the channel selection itself. As we have noted, a sensitive communicator will consider carefully decisions as to when to place a phone call, when to conduct face-to-face interviews, when to send a memo. As listeners, we may respond consciously or unconsciously to these channels. Some individuals may have an aversion to the telephone, for example, as an invasion of privacy. Indeed, the telephone can be obtrusive. A person standing in line at a ticket window may have to wait longer while the clerk handles telephone calls, which take precedence when the callers interrupt the clerk.

The channels we select relate to the environment (physical setting) in which we communicate. Again, elements in the setting can enhance or can detract from the communication. We can exercise some control over the lighting, ventilation, seating arrangements, and even room colors. But a failure in electrical power, for instance, could darken the room and end the communication.

Communication as a Simultaneous Process

While all of these variables have an influence—positively or negatively—on the outcome of the communication, we can work to maintain some control over them and make an effort to facilitate the process. Throughout our communication efforts, it is helpful for us, as listeners, to keep in perspective that communication

Within most communication
transactions, we simultaneously serve
as sources and receivers.
Photo by Robert Tocha.

is symbolic and that it is a process. As we have noted, our language system comprises symbolic words and nonverbal dimensions which we utilize to *represent* the ideas we are expressing. And we are constantly involved in a process of encoding and decoding messages in a fairly simultaneous sequence. We really function as source and receiver at one and the same time—sending messages and receiving/decoding the feedback from the listener. And the listener, in turn, receives/decodes the message and, simultaneously, sends/encodes feedback messages.[3] This simultaneous process suggests that we, ideally, ought to view the source and receiver as communicators, not separately delineating the roles.[4] Thus, a model of the communication process might more realistically depict this simultaneous role-taking:[5]

This perspective of communication as the simultaneous role-taking of source and receiver has come to be known as a *transactional* perspective. The view suggests that communication is more than the interaction of a source and a receiver and that, indeed, we function as communicators in the process in encoding and decoding the messages. This simultaneous process, then, suggests that we do not serve as just a source or a receiver but that, rather, we serve both functions within most communication transactions.

If you communicate with your professor in the classroom, for example, you may receive his or her lecture on intrapersonal communication and, at the same

Figure 2.2.
Transactional model of
communication.

ENVIRONMENT

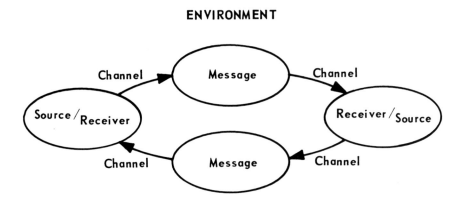

time, send him or her feedback through your nonverbal language that you agree, approve, support what the professor is telling the class about intrapersonal communication. As the professor develops the lecture, he or she should "read" the feedback he or she is receiving from you and your classmates and adapt the lecture accordingly.

While such a view of the communication process is an important perspective to understand the complexities of our roles as communicators, it is necessary to study the communication skills involved from a more distinct source and/or receiver perspective. And it is the focus of this book to examine the listening skills involved in the receiving process.

Implications for the Listener

The transactional perspective of the process of communication, then, is a useful perspective for the listener. It is helpful to remember that, as a communicator, the listener is actively involved in receiving and sending (decoding and encoding) messages. While we listen to the verbal and the nonverbal messages of a speaker, we send verbal and nonverbal feedback messages back to our fellow communicators. And we send these messages through our perceptual filters—the frame of reference which is made up of our background, experience, knowledge, attitudes, and communication skills. These variables affect our efficiency and our effectiveness in decoding and encoding the messages as we handle them simultaneously.

The listener, to be effective, must develop a clear understanding of his or her frame of reference in order to know what perceptual filters are influencing his or her responses to messages. And the effective listener will develop the necessary listening skills in order to decode the messages and in order to encode feedback messages which will be appropriate to the communication.

Summary

In this chapter, we have examined the components of the communication process—source, message, channel, receiver, feedback, noise, and environment. These elements are affected by variables which facilitate or distort the communication process, depending largely on how effectively the communicators are able to control them. Such variables as communicator skills, attitudes, and knowledge combine with message structure and code and channel dimensions to complicate the communication process. Throughout, it is useful to keep the perspective that communication is symbolic (that we use verbal and nonverbal language to symbolically *represent* our ideas) and that it is an ongoing, transactional *process* in which source and receiver simultaneously encode and decode messages.

Activities to Try

1. Design your own model of the communication process. Incorporate the components of communication and the variables which you think are important to the process. Attempt to illustrate the simultaneous nature of the source and receiver functions within the process.
2. Illustrate the process of communication with a real-life situation in which you describe a particular incident in which comunication variables played a major role in the outcome of the communication.
3. Make a list of barriers to effective communication. Illustrate these barriers with examples from your own communication experience.

Notes

1. For a detailed discussion of variables influencing the communication process, you might like to read David K. Berlo, *The Process of Communication* (New York: Holt, Rinehart and Winston, 1960).
2. This is the perspective held by semanticists, who argue that "words don't mean; people do." See, for instance, S. I. Hayakawa, *Language in Thought and Action* (New York: Harcourt, Brace and World, 1949).
3. An early proponent of this view was Wilbur Schramm in "How Communication Works," *The Process and Effects of Mass Communication* (Urbana: University of Illinois Press, 1955), pp. 3–26.

4. For a discussion of this perspective, see Roy M. Berko, Andrew D. Wolvin, and Darlyn R. Wolvin, *Communicating: A Social and Career Focus* (Boston: Houghton Mifflin Company, 1977), pp. 17–18.

5. One of the earliest communication scholars to develop a model of communication from a transactional perspective was Wilbur Schramm in "How Communication Works," *The Process and Effects of Mass Communication,* pp. 4–8.

concepts you will encounter

Distinct Behavior
Listening Construct
Auding
Structural Approach
Aural Stimuli
Visual Stimuli
Components
Receiving
Otitis Media
Otosclerosis
Sensorineural Impairment
Presbycusis
Sociocusus
Binaural Hearing
Masking
Auditory Fatigue
Attending To
Selective Attention
Filter Theory
General Arousal
Energetic Attention
Scanning
Long-Term Memory System
Short-Term Memory System
Rehearsal

Fluctuating Attention
Assigning Meaning
Meaning as a Behavioral
    Disposition
Categorical System
Referent
Attributes
Criterial Attributes
Noncriterial Attributes
Single Attribute Category
Disjunctive Category
Relational Category
Conjunctive Category
Formal Attributes
Functional Attributes
Incorrect Categorization
Remembering
Responding
Overt Responses
Covert Responses
Agreement
Creative Listening
Purposeful Listening
Dynamic Process

the process of listening

3

In chapter 2, we stressed that communication is an ongoing, transactional process involving both the sending and the receiving of messages. Although we will focus only on the receptive aspect of the communication process in this chapter, we must keep the perspective that even though listening is—in itself—a process, it is also an integral part of the total communication process.

The Nature of Listening as a Distinct Behavior

Basic to any attempt made to define listening is the answer to this question: Is listening a distinct behavior that is separate from other intellectual behaviors? Several factor studies—including those conducted by Caffrey, Caffrey and Smith, Karlin, and Hanley—have provided evidence that listening is a distinct activity.[1] However, the factor analysis that has given decisive support that there is a separate listening factor was performed by Spearritt in Australia.[2] The main hypothesis that Spearritt tested was formally stated as follows: "The variance of listening comprehension tests can be accounted for by reasoning, verbal comprehension, attention and memory factors, and no separate listening factor need be postulated."[3] To test this hypothesis, Spearritt employed a battery of thirty-four tests designed to measure reasoning (inductive, deductive, and general), verbal comprehension, attention, auditory resistance, memory (span, rote, and meaningful), and listening comprehension. The nine listening tests used were either specially designed or modified for the investigation; one test was an adaptation of the *Sequential Tests of Educational Progress: Listening Comprehension* (STEP), three were prepared tests based on short talks (one designed to appeal to both sexes, one designed to appeal to boys but not girls, and one designed to appeal to girls but not boys), one was a prepared test designed to represent everyday conversation or spontaneous discussion, and four were reading tests presented orally. The test battery was initially administered to over 400 sixth graders in ten schools in Melbourne; the final sample consisted of 161 boys and 139 girls, for whom results on all tests were available. Spearritt clearly isolated a separate listening comprehension factor, and, thus, the hypothesis was rejected.

   The studies that we have cited here—especially Spearritt's study—seem "to show that listening is a kind of human behavior in itself, separate from reading, from memory, and from other intellectual behaviors, although dependent on them as they are probably dependent on it."[4] Having provided evidence that listening is a distinct activity, we will now define this activity.

A Definition of Listening

The definition of listening is still in the process of being developed. Among the factors contributing to this delay are the following: listening is a complex, covert act difficult to investigate; much research in listening has not been coordinated or collated; and research in listening is in an exploratory state—with most of the research on listening having been conducted in the past four decades.

Despite these and other factors, many of which current researchers and members of the newly established International Listening Association (ILA) are considering, a number of definitions have been suggested. The earliest of the definitions cited in this chapter is dated 1925; the most recent is dated 1979. During the evolution of a listening definition, differences have emerged—differences in the processes or elements encompassed, terms used, symbols included, and specifications made. These various definitions have often been based mainly upon speculations, some more reasonable—in the light of present knowledge—than others. Nevertheless, they have all—whether by raising questions, stimulating research, and/or adding ideas—contributed to the framework of a listening construct.

Proposed Definitions

Some of the proposed definitions of listening that have led to our current understanding of this complex act are the following:

. . . an analysis of the impressions resulting from concentration where an effort of will is required—Tucker (1925)[5]

. . . the ability to understand spoken language—Rankin (1926)[6]

. . . the conscious, purposeful registration of sounds upon the mind [which] leads to further mental activity . . . all true listening is creative—Hook (1950)[7]

. . . the ability to understand and respond effectively to oral communication—Johnson (1951)[8]

. . . the process of reacting to, interpreting, and relating the spoken language in terms of past experiences and further courses of action—Barbe and Meyers (1954)[9]

. . . the aural assimilation of spoken symbols in a face-to-face speaker-audience situation, with both oral and visual cues present—Brown and Carlsen (1955)[10]

. . . the capacity of an individual to understand spoken language in the presence of a speaker—Still (1955)[11]

. . . a selective process by which sounds communicated by some source are received, critically interpreted, and acted upon by a purposeful listener—Jones (1956)[12]

. . . a definite, usually voluntary, effort to apprehend accoustically—Barbara (1957)[13]

. . . the act of giving attention to the spoken word, not only in hearing symbols, but in the reacting with understanding—Hampleman (1958)[14]

. . . the process of hearing, identifying, understanding and interpreting spoken language—Lewis (1958)[15]

. . . the composite process by which oral language communicated by some source is received, critically and purposefully attended to, recognized, and interpreted (or comprehended) in terms of past experiences and future expectancies—Petrie (1961)[16]

. . . the selective process of attending to, hearing, understanding, and remembering aural symbols—Barker (1971)[17]

. . . the process by which spoken language is converted to meaning in the mind—Lundsteen (1971)[18]

. . . a process that takes place when a human organism receives data orally—Weaver (1972)[19]

. . . the process whereby the human ear receives sound stimuli from other people and through a series of steps interprets the sound stimuli in the brain and remembers it—Hirsch (1979)[20]

Questions Crucial to the Construction of a Listening Definition

A quick glance at these definitions shows us that listening scholars do not agree on what listening is. A more careful study of these definitions, however, will reveal to us that they raise many questions that are crucial for us to answer if we are to construct a definition of listening. Among the most critical questions are the following:

1. In the various definitions, what different terms are used? Which of these terms are synonymous?
2. Should both verbal and nonverbal symbols be included in a listening definition? Is there a visual factor involved in listening? Is the visual factor a necessary component of the listening act?
3. Can listening occur only in face-to-face situations?
4. What processes or elements are encompassed in the listening act?
5. Is hearing a component of listening, or is it only a necessary condition?
6. Is listening more than the mere perception of sound?
7. Does listening require conscious effort?
8. Is retention a necessary component of the listening act?
9. Is reacting and responding a necessary component of listening? Must the reaction be overt? Can it be only covert?
10. Is listening creative? If so, in what ways is it creative?
11. Is listening purposeful? If so, what are the purposes of listening?

12. Is listening a process?

In this chapter, we will answer these crucial questions.

Differences in Proposed Definitions

As we carefully study the proposed definitions, we find numerous differences in the authors' assignment of meaning to the term *listening*. One major difference is the elements or processes that are mentioned: analyzing, concentrating, understanding, registering, converting meaning to the mind, engaging in further mental activity, responding, reacting, interpreting, relating to past experiences and future expectancies, assimilating, acting upon, selecting, receiving, apprehending, attending, hearing, remembering, identifying, recognizing, and comprehending. In naming the processes or elements involved in the listening act, it is also apparent that there are differences in the terms used. The fact that synonyms, such as *responding* and *reacting* and *understanding* and *comprehending,* are frequently used calls further attention to the need for a more specific definition.

Additionally, writers differ concerning the types of symbols to which the listener attends. The majority of the authors have emphasized that listening involves attending to verbal sounds only as is indicated by again synonymous phrases such as "spoken language," "spoken symbols," "oral communication," "oral language," "aural symbols," and "the spoken word." On the other hand, Tucker, Hook, Jones, Barbara, and Weaver include nonverbal stimuli as well.

Brown, observing such disagreements and verbal confusion, recognized the need for a more precise term to denote listening to verbal material. He proposed that the term *auding* be used to designate the comprehension of verbal sounds. A definition of reading—the other receptive language art skill—provided the key to the definition of auding; he defined auding as "the gross process of listening to, recognizing, and interpreting spoken symbols."[21] Brown, distinguishing between listening and auding, stated that "listening is a factor in auding precisely as looking is a factor in reading, that auding is confined to language whereas listening is not, and that listening, even when earnestly applied, to unfamiliar language is not enough."[22] Apparently, to Brown, listening is "paying attention to the sounds."[23]

Although Caffrey, Furness, Horrworth, and others have adopted the term *auding* and have limited their definitions to the inclusion of spoken words only, their definitions of auding differ. Caffrey defines auding as "the process of hearing, listening to, recognizing, and interpreting or comprehending spoken language."[24] Furness describes auding as consisting "of at least six processes: (a) hearing, (b) listening, (c) recognizing spoken language, (d) interpreting oral symbols, (e) supplementing meaning and knowledge of the symbols, and (f) being aware of facts or assumptions not uttered."[25] Horrworth expresses her interpretation of the findings of Brown, Caffrey, Furness, and others in the following paradigm: "Auding = Hearing + Listening + Cognizing." She further defines hearing as "the process by which sound waves are received, modified, and relayed along the nervous system by the ear"; listening as "the process of directing attention to and thereby becoming aware of sound sequences"; and cognition as "a generic term used often to denote all of the various aspects of knowing, including perception, judgment, reasoning, remembering; and thinking and imagining."[26]

We believe that despite the frequent misuse of the term *listening*, the term is too fully established in our culture for listening researchers to attempt to change its name. Rather than using *auding* or coining a new term, we prefer to strive to clarify the term with which society is already familiar.

In addition to the limitations some writers have placed upon the symbols attended to in the listening act, other specifications have been made. Brown and Carlsen and Still stipulate that listening must be face-to-face. Brown and Carlsen also include visual cues as factors in listening. Furthermore, the viewpoint that listening requires purpose, creativity, and effort are expressed. And, beginning with the definition of Barbe and Meyers, the term *process* is frequently included. These specifications will be discussed later is this chapter.

New Directions toward a Unified Definition of Listening

It is apparent that researchers in the field of listening have employed varied definitions since 1925. Recent advancements, however, have been and are being made toward the elimination of the major factors that have contributed to the delay of a unified construct of listening.

The quantity of research in listening is steadily growing. This growth can be evidenced by the amount of listening research cited in reviews, bibliographies, indexes and books. Although the quality of the research is sometimes held suspect, new directions are being taken to improve the quality.

The coordination and collation of listening research appears to offer the most promise toward the improvement of the quality of the research as well as the development of a listening construct. The newly formed International Listening Association (1979) has as one of its primary goals the establishing of a clearinghouse to allow the professional interchange of listening materials and research findings. Both the National Center for Educational Research and Development (NCERD) and the National Institute of Education (NIE) have already made contributions toward alleviating the problem of uncollated research. Both government agencies have directed the separate Educational Resources Information Center (ERIC) Clearinghouses to commission from recognized authorities information analysis papers in specific areas. Two ERIC Clearinghouses—the Clearinghouse on the Teaching of English and the Clearinghouse on Reading and Communication Skills—and the National Council of Teachers of English (NCTE) and the Speech Communication Association (SCA) have worked jointly with the government agencies and published works in the area of listening. Under the sponsorship of NCTE/ERIC, Lundsteen wrote a state-of-the-art monograph on listening in 1971. In this book, she analyzes and synthesizes published and unpublished material on listening. Under the sponsorship of SCA/ERIC, Wolvin and Coakley wrote a listening booklet in 1979; this booklet blends theory and research in listening with classroom practices for improving listening. In both works, the authors devote many pages to defining listening. Recognizing that not all of the questions are answerable as yet, Lundsteen prefaces her discussion of a definition of listening with the following remark: "Defining listening is a challenge. There are many unknowns in this problem calling for creativity and commitment to go beyond what is presented here."[27] Although, as Lundsteen has stated, many problems in defining listening still exist, progress toward developing a concept of listening is being made.

Aspects Encompassed in the Listening Process

Drawing on research findings in the field of listening and related fields, we will now present our definition of listening. In an attempt to avoid the confusion that often results from defining a complex skill in a single sentence, we will first present a detailed discussion of what listening is—as it is currently believed to be—and then we will present our definition of listening. Although there are many approaches that can be used when one is defining listening, we have chosen to use the structural approach; that is, our definition will answer the question, "What are the aspects encompassed in the listening process?"

Stimuli

First, we will seek to clarify what kinds of stimuli are involved in the act of listening.

Aural Stimuli. Although many definers of listening have limited the symbols attended to in the listening act to spoken words, Weaver includes verbal data (words), vocal data (voice cues, such as inflections), and other kinds of sounds (nonlinguistic sounds) as types of aurally input data to which the listener attends and assigns meaning.[28] We support Weaver's view; the listener attends and assigns meaning to a shrilly screamed exclamation, "The house is on fire!", as well as to the sound of a smoke alarm.

Visual Stimuli. Must both the receiver and the sender be present in a face-to-face situation for listening to occur? We agree with those who believe that listening can occur without the listener seeing the message originator; one can engage in the listening act, for example, by way of television, public address system, intercom, and other communication mediums. However, we must point out that what we see (or "what we listen to with the third ear") can contribute to our listening effectiveness. When we consider Birdwhistell's findings that spoken words account for no more than 30 to 35 percent of all social interactions and Mehrabian's estimates that as much as 93 percent of a message's total meaning may stem from nonverbal cues, we realize that visual cues can assist us in assigning meaning.[29] However, visual cues are not necessary components of the listening act—as those who are blind can readily confirm.

Components

Now, let us determine what processes or elements are encompassed in the listening act.

Receiving. The first component, receiving, refers to the physiological process of hearing and/or seeing aural and/or visual stimuli (phonemes, words, vocal cues, nonlinguistic sounds, nonverbal cues).

The Seeing Process. The seeing process begins wih light rays—reflected from an object—falling on the cornea in the front of the eye (fig. 3.1). The cornea is made up of tough, transparent tissue with no blood vessels. The rays then pass through the liquid *aqueous humor* contained in the anterior chamber directly behind the cornea. The rays proceed through the lens and the vitreous humor behind the lens. The cornea and the lens are separated by the iris which contains the pupil, an opening that can vary in diameter from approximately two to eight milimeters. The constriction of the pupil can improve the quality of the image formed and increase the depth of focus of the eye.

Once the light rays pass through the lens, they fall on the retina, the innermost part of the eyeball. The retina contains, at the back, the receptors which are sensitive to light. To reach these receptors, the rays pass back and forth across the surface of the retina, containing the optic nerve fibers.

The optic nerve fibers pass through the back of the eye to the optic thalamus and on to the visual cortex, the visual center of the brain. These fibers are set into stimulation throughout the system by the light rays.[30]

The Hearing Process. The process of hearing is complicated by the intricacies of the hearing mechanism. Sound waves are received by the ear and transmitted to the brain. The outer ear (fig. 3.2), which consists of the pinna and the canal, serves to direct the sound waves into the hearing mechanism. The pinna, the prominent part of the outer ear, serves only this purpose, while in other forms of animals the pinna—having the ability to move—can play a greater role in detecting and directing sounds. A dog, for instance, can move his ears to localize sounds. The external canal of the outer ear is a passage which may be a bit over one inch in length. It contains hairs and wax to protect the eardrum from penetration of dirt and objects.

The middle ear connects the eardrum with the ossicular chain containing the smallest bones in the body—the hammer (malleus), the anvil (incus) and the stirrup (stapes). These bones connect the eardrum to the opening of the inner ear, the oval window. The middle ear also includes the Eustachian tube which serves as an equalizer of air pressure and, thus, enables the middle ear to compensate for external air pressure.

The inner ear serves as the final organ for hearing *and* as the sensory organ for balance. The balance results from the vestibular apparatus containing the utricle, saccule, and semicircular canals. The hearing part of the inner ear is the cochlea, which resembles a snail shell. The entire inner ear is filled with fluid. The cochlear duct, containing this fluid, includes the organ of corti, the end organ of hearing. This organ consists of four or five rows of hair cells which connect

Figure 3.1.
Anatomy of the human ear.
Reprinted, by permission, from Zenetron
Inc.

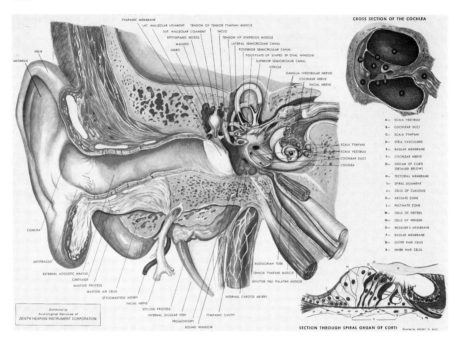

Figure 3.2.
Anatomy of the eye.
Reprinted, by permission, from CIBA
Pharmaceutical Company.

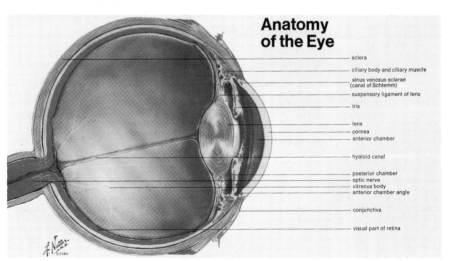

with nerve fibers which run into the center of the cochlea and form the cochlear branch of the VIIIth nerve (the auditory nerve). This branch joins the vestibular branch, and the VIIIth nerve proceeds to the brain stem and the cerebral cortex.

Normally we hear by air conduction since most sounds are air born and since the air conduction mechanism is more sensitive than the mechanism of bone conduction. The sound waves, channeled through the external meatus, set the eardrum into vibration. The ossicular chain, connected by the hammer to the eardrum, is then set into vibration. The three tiny bones of the ossicular chain vibrate as a unit and produce a rocking motion of the stapes in the oval window, matching the sound waves of the air to that of the fluid. The fluid of the oval window then leads to a bulging outward of the round window, transmitted through the cochlear duct. The bulging leads to movement of the membrane, initiating nerve impulses carried to the cochlear portion of the VIIIth nerve and then to the cerebral cortex which hears the vibrations set in motion on the eardrum. The ear responds to a band of frequencies (measured by hertz, Hz) and to intensity (measured by decibels, dB). Normal speech is in the range of 400–4000 Hz and 60 dB.

Various theories of hearing attempt to explain how an individual, through this process, can discriminate pitches—the frequency (as measured by hertz, Hz) of sound. One theory, the Place theory, suggests that the cochlea resembles a spiral which is tuned to different pitch levels with the vibrations on this elastic membrane varying with the size of the diameter of the spiral. This idea, popularized by the German scientist Helmholz, holds that the base end of the cochlea, then, is sensitive to high frequencies, and the other end is stimulated by low frequencies.

An alternative theory of hearing explains pitch perception as the result of the frequency of occurrence of impulses in the auditory nerve. George von Bekesy, a Nobel prizewinning scientist who has spent years researching the hearing mechanism, speculates that the sound results from a wave traveling from the base to the apex of the cochlea.[31]

The complex process of hearing, which may never be fully understood by scientists, is made all the more complicated with malfunctions to the hearing mechanism. The most common problem results from the blockage of the outer ear by an excessive accumulation of wax. The inner ear may become inflamed or infested (otitis media), often the result of a respiratory infection. At times, cases of otitis media may become chronic, particularly in younger children. Treating otitis media requires antibiotic drug therapy or a simple myringotomy, a surgical process of making an incision in the eardrum and inserting a small tube to allow the middle ear to drain.

Less common is a congenital condition known as otosclerosis, a progressive disease which turns the hard bone of the inner ear into spongy bone matter. For some unknown reason, the disease primarily affects Caucasian women. A new surgical technique, stapedectomy, consists of removing the stapes completely and creating a prosthetic link between the incus and the oval window. This technique has been found to restore hearing to within 10dB.

Some individuals suffer sensorineural impairment. In this condition, the sound is conducted properly to the fluid in the inner ear, but it cannot be perceived normally. The sensorineural impairment, in its extreme, leads to partial or complete deafness. Those individuals with a slight sensorineural loss may be prone to "shouting" in order to hear themselves as well as others. Other than attempting to arrest further sensory loss, most hearing specialists feel it is not very possible to restore sensory loss once the nerve fibers in the cochlea or in the VIIIth nerve are destroyed.

The sensorineural impairment of the hearing function relates, in part, to the physical deterioration of the hearing mechanism through increased age. The progressive hearing loss is known as presbycusis. The process starts at about the age of twenty and becomes increasingly prevalent with each decade of an individual's life span.[32]

In addition to presbycusis, all persons are affected by sociocusis—hearing loss from exposure to nonoccupational noise sources such as rock'n'roll music and jet plane flyovers. The influence of noise pollution continues to be a major environmental problem in the United States. The Public Health Service, for example, conducted a study of some of the common environmental sound levels (measured by decibels, dB, on the A-network of a sound level meter, abbreviated as dBA) of noises, and the findings are reported in table 3.1.[33]

The federal Environmental Protection Agency is charged with controlling noise pollution through the Noise Control Act of 1972. This legislation mandates the EPA to identify and regulate major sources of noise and to label noisy products. In addition, the agency attempts to coordinate noise control efforts of state and local governments through the Quiet Communities Act of 1978.[34]

One local government that has been successful in noise control is the Seattle, Washington, government. In only one year, 1980, Seattle banished outdoor rock concerts from the Seattle Center, forced a large dairy to install quieter refrigeration units on its delivery trucks, required owners of heat pumps to enclose them in soundproof cases, and stopped the National Oceanographic and Atmospheric Administration from night dredging on Lake Washington. Curt Honrer, Seattle's noise abatement coordinator, feels that the program has had a psychological spin-off: "The people themselves have more awareness of noise. They value their quiet."[35]

Despite these advances, enforcement of noise standards is difficult because few agencies can support the vast number of inspectors that would be required. Consequently, greater public awareness of the real problem with noise pollution and its effect on our physical and psychological system may be an important key to dealing with the situation.

Hearing hygiene, it would seem, extends beyond care of the hearing mechanism through proper cleanliness and medical attention as necessary. Avoidance of exposure to noise sources is a further dimension of proper care of the hearing system. This proper care of the system, of course, supports effective listening behavior.

Table 3.1. 'A' weighted sound levels of some noises found in different environments

Sound Level, dBA	Industrial (and Military)	Community (or Outdoor)	Home (or Indoor)
—130—	Armored Personnel Carrier (123 dB)		
—120— Uncomfortably Loud	Oxygen Torch (121 dB) Scraper-Loader (117 dB)		
—110—	Compactor (116 dB)		Rock'N'Roll Band (108–114 dB)
—100—Very Loud	Riveting Machine (110 dB) Textile Loom (106 dB)	Jet Flyover @ 100 ft. (103 dB) Power Mower (96 dB)	
— 90—	Electric Furnace Area (100 dB)	Compressor @ 20 ft. (94 dB)	Inside Subway Car-35 mph (95 dB)
— 80— Moderately Loud	Farm Tractor (98 dB) Newspaper Press (97 dB)	Rock Drill @ 100 ft. (92 dB)	Cockpit-Light Aircraft (90 dB)
— 70—	Cockpit-Prop Aircraft (88 dB)	Motorcycles @ 25 ft. (90 dB) Propeller Aircraft	Food Blender (88 dB) Garbage Disposal (80 dB)
— 60—	Milling Machine (85 dB)	Flyover @ 1000 ft. (88 dBA)	Clothes Washer (78 dB)
— 50—Quiet	Cotton Spinning (83 dB)	Diesel Truck, 40 mph @ 50 ft. (84 dB)	Living Room Music (76 dB)
— 40—	Lathe (81 dB) Tabulating (80 dB)	Diesel Train, 40–50 mph @ 100 ft. (83 dB)	Dishwasher (75 dB)
— 30—Very Quiet		Passenger Car, 65 mph @ 25 ft. (77 dB)	TV-Audio (70 dB) Vacuum (70 dB) Conversation (60 dB)
— 20—			
— 10—Just Audible		Near Freeway-Auto Traffic (64 dB) Air-Conditioning Unit @ 20 ft. (60 dB)	
— 0—Threshold of Hearing (1000–4000 Hz)		Large Transformer @ 200 ft. (53 dB) Light Traffic @ 100 ft. (50 dB)	

Note: Unless otherwise specified, listed sound levels are measured at typical operator-listener distances from source. Noise readings taken from general acoustical literature and observations by PHS.

There are three additional factors that weaken the hearing process. One is binaural hearing problems—a lack of coordinated functioning of both ears and, thus, the inability to discriminate the direction of the source of the sound. Another factor is masking—the existence of background noise or other types of interference (such as conflicting simultaneous messages) while the individual is attempting to hear the intended oral message. A third problem is that of auditory fatigue—fatigue from continuous exposure to sounds of certain frequency, such as a monotonous or droning voice, a ticking clock, a running appliance, and a

Our receiving of aural stimuli is often
affected by noise sources.
Photo by Robert Tocha.

dripping faucet. If any of these factors are operating, the process of hearing is weakened, and, thus, listening is impeded.

Is hearing an aspect or component of listening, or is hearing, like consciousness, only a necessary condition? A person who is totally deaf cannot listen because he cannot hear; therefore, hearing is a necessary condition. However, since *listening* and *hearing* are so frequently misused as synonyms, most listening scholars, including us, believe that hearing is an integral component of the listening process.

Attending to. The second component, attending to, refers to the focused perception of selected stimuli. This act embraces the moment before and during the reception of a potential stimulus.[36]

At any moment, numerous stimuli in our immediate environment are vying for our attention. These stimuli may be external, such as a speaker's words, a noise in the hall, a poster on the wall, or an attractive person in the room; or they may be internal, such as a headache, a distracting thought, or a numb foot. Suppose you are listening to a student speak in the classroom. The speaker's message is the stimulus you have selected to attend to. However, outside you hear a motor rev and shouts of other students; internally you feel hunger pains or have an itch. So what do you do? Can you divide your attention energy among several stimuli? If so, how many stimuli can you attend to at any given time?

Selective Attention. There is a number of stimuli to which we can attend at any one time.[37] However, there is no limit to the number of stimuli constantly competing for our attention. If all stimuli seeking our attention at any given instant were sent to the cortex, a neural overload would result. Thus, we must constantly engage in a process of selecting only those stimuli to which we will attend. It is believed that some discriminatory mechanism assists us in selecting the wanted from the unwanted aural stimuli.

Many explanations of how this discriminatory process occurs have been proposed. Among others, the following scholars have studied this phenomenon: Broadbent, Deutsch and Deutsch, and Treisman.

Broadbent has proposed a "filter theory." According to this model of attention, aural stimuli enter the nervous system through a number of input channels which include, among others, verbal classes, languages, and position in auditory space. Broadbent contends that the various input lines converge onto a filter that functions as a selective mechanism. The filter selects stimuli on the basis of certain features toward which it is biased, and it allows the selected stimuli to penetrate to consciousness. Unselected stimuli are held in the short-term memory store for a brief period of time.[38]

Deutsch and Deutsch have found Broadbent's theory to be attractive when applied to simple and few discriminations. They have questioned its application, however, to cases where complex and many discriminations are needed. Thus, they have proposed the following model:

> Another mechanism is proposed, which assumes the existence of a shifting reference standard, which takes up the level of the most important arriving signal. . . . Only the most important signals coming in will be acted on or remembered. On the other hand, more important signals than those present at an immediately preceding time will be able to break in, for these will raise the height of the level and so displace the previously most important signals as the highest.[39]

Deutsch and Deutsch also discuss the role of general arousal in selective attention. They believe that some degree of general arousal is necessary for attention to operate. When aroused, an individual will attend to any incoming stimulus provided that it is not accompanied by a more important one. When asleep, however, an individual will respond to only very "important" messages (such as a person's own name or the cry of a mother's infant).[40] Experimental studies conducted by Moray, Oswald, Taylor, and Treisman, and Howarth and Ellis have indicated that some selective mechanism functions when a person recognizes his or her own name (an "important" word) during dichotic listening, during sleep, and during normal listening under noise.[41] Treisman has suggested that such "important" words and, perhaps, danger signals "have permanently lower thresholds for activation or are more readily available than others . . . others would be lowered temporarily by incoming signals on some kind of conditional probability basis. . . ."[42]

The third model of attention has been proposed by Treisman. She contends that messages—having arrived to some part of the nervous system over different input channels—are first analyzed for physical characteristics such as pitch, loudness, and location in space. A filter uses the information obtained by this analysis to identify the messages to be selected. Other messages proceed to a pattern recognizer which handles complex discrimination (the analysis of meaning). The pattern recognizer consists of recognizers or dictionary units of known words. The units have different thresholds for activation. If the input data are intense enough to pass the thresholds of the appropriate recognizers, the listener then will be consciously aware of the verbal stimuli.[43]

Although, presently, disagreements exist as to how selective attention operates, where discriminatory decisions are made, and what happens to unselected stimuli, there is experimental evidence, as has been cited previously, that attention is selective. As listeners, we base our selection of aural stimuli upon a priority system that exists within each of us. Bartlett has made reference to how selective attention relates to the listener's perception: "Selective listening is determined mainly by the qualitative differences of stimuli in relation to predispositions—cognitive, affective, and motor—of the listener."[44]

Energetic Attention. Not only is attention selective, but also it is energetic. It requires both effort and desire. Although we can divide our attention, we can give complete attention to only one stimulus at a time. If we expend too much energy on too many stimuli, we will no longer be attending; instead, we will be scanning (that is, sweeping the perceptual field to discover that which should be attended to).[45] Thus, by concentrating our attention energy on one stimulus instead of on many, we can focus more sharply upon the selected stimulus.

Once we have selected a stimulus to which we will attend, it has our attention; that is, we become aware of it, and we further process it. There is some evidence, however, that some stimuli that seem never to be attended to (or of which the individual seems never to be aware) enter and remain in the memory system.[46] Generally, though, only stimuli that have been attended to enter the memory system.

The memory system referred to in the previous paragraph is the long-term memory system (LTM). Most researchers posit that there are two memory systems—the short-term memory system (STM) and the LTM.[47] The STM refers to the current contents of a person's awareness (such as a telephone number that is remembered until it can be dialed), and the LTM refers to everything else in a person's memory system. A principal difference between the two memory systems is that the "STM has a fixed capacity that is subject to overload and consequently loss of elements stored in it . . . while LTM is, in effect, infinitely expansible."[48] Norman believes that the STM is probably limited to holding three or four items and that items decay after a lapse of twenty seconds.[49] Other scholars, including Posner, believe that data can remain in the STM without decaying up to a minute.[50] The function of the STM can be illustrated in a simplified manner. Suppose you are attending a party where you know very few of the other guests. If you are introduced to several people in succession, your STM is presented with the names of Jim and Steve before you have learned the names of Susan and Shirley. The new names tend to push the former names out of your STM. Unless you quickly transfer each name to the LTM, you most likely will lose the name. However, the data in the STM may be preserved longer and, thus, move to the LTM if they go through rehearsal. Rehearsal—the repetition of data by way of covert speech or concentration on data—appears to increase the chances of stimuli reaching the cortext for attention.[51] So, if you concentrate while you repeat each name as you meet each person, the chances are greater that each name will reach the LTM. In general, only those stimuli that have been attended to reach the LTM. Thus, for listening to occur, the listener must attend to the aural stimuli and then search the LTM in order to process the input data further.

Fluctuating Attention. Relevant also to the listening act is an understanding of the waning of attention. We cannot pay attention to the selected stimulus for as long as we desire. Attention fluctuates. The fading of attention is sometimes not caused by distraction; instead, attention fades because of a succession of lapses that Haider has termed "microsleep." Thus, periodically, our attention energy will wane because we are "asleep."[52] At other times, though, when our attention wanes, it is not due to "sleep"; instead, it is due to our short attention spans or our lack of effort. We can, however, increase the length of our attention span "through concentration, practice, and self-discipline."[53]

From this explanation of the process of attending to, we can see that if we have a questionable priority system upon which we base our selection of stimuli, a lack of motivation to concentrate, and/or a limited attention span, our listening efficiency will be diminished.

Just as *hearing* (for example, "You don't hear a word I say!") and *listening* are often erroneously used as synonyms, *attending* (for example, "Can't you pay attention to what I say?") and *listening* are often incorrectly equated. The listening process encompasses more than the two processes of receiving and attending. We can, for example, hear and attend to a foreign language, but if we cannot assign meaning to the aural stimuli, we have not engaged in the total listening process.

Assigning Meaning. The third component, assigning meaning, refers to the interpretation or understanding of the stimuli heard and/or seen and attended to. In this process, the listener's goal is to attach meaning as similar as possible to that intended by the message sender; however, we must realize that assigning meaning is a very personal process, and, thus, due to the senders' and receivers' differences in past experiences, present feelings, and even future expectancies, we often do not reach the desired goal.

Theories on How Meaning Is Assigned. Various theories have been posited as to how meaning is assigned. Among these theories are the image theory, classical conditioning, linguistic reference, meaning as an implicit response, meaning as a mediating response, and meaning as a behavioral disposition.[54]

Lundsteen appears to favor the image theory. Utilizing evidence established by memory research and theories proposed by Anderson,[55] she suggests that listeners go through two separate processes: "acoustical encoding" (the trans-

lation of the aural data into internal speech) and "semantic encoding" (the translation of the aural data into tentative, perceptual images or internal pictures).[56] After having formed these initial images, we search through images held in our memory store in order to find possible "matches" for the data. We may then compare the cues we have selected with previous knowledge and experience so that we can form further tentative images. If we have not found a "match" yet, we may test our cues by questioning and summarizing, or we may return to our memory store for further search. Once we have matched the cues with the aural input by way of forming tentative images, searching, comparing, testing, and decoding, we get meaning. We then decide what the aural stimuli means to us.[57]

Although Barker does not elaborate upon how meaning is assigned, he briefly states that there are two levels of meaning. The first level, the primary meaning assignment, is associated with the classical conditioning responses to the aural stimuli. After integrating past experience with this primary meaning, however, listeners arrive at a secondary meaning. This is the meaning listeners believe was intended by the message sender.[58]

Weaver supports—with slight modification—the theory of meaning as a behavioral disposition.[59] This theory is based upon a system of categories into which the mind sorts and assigns aural stimuli. Although the system was devised by Bruner, Goodnow, and Austin in 1956,[60] Brown made the categorical system widely known.[61] Categories are stored in the memory. After we have selected an aural stimulus for attention (for instance, *bicuspid*), we search our memory to find the category in which this stimulus "fits" (where memories of other stimuli with a similar pattern are stored). We cannot assign meaning until we have found a "match." Having found the "match" (*tooth,* in our example), we then ascribe meaning (know approximately what the stimulus means) because of the category evoked; the stimulus then assumes the meaning of the category (in this case, a *double-pointed jaw tooth*).

The memory system has thousands of categories. Each word and each recurrence in the nonlinguistic world has a referent; each referent is a category. Also, in itself, the name of each referent is a category. Brown exemplifies this last statement by citing the following: At the beginning of a course, an instructor generally uses many new words. When the instructor first uses a new word, he or she establishes a new category to be filled in with later experience. At first, the category is empty because nothing is signaled by the new word except the existence of a category.[62]

Each category, "a human construction imposed on an array of objects or events,"[63] has characteristic features called attributes. An attribute is "any dimension on which objects and events can differ."[64] Attributes are criterial (essential) and noncriterial (nonessential). When we use some value of an attribute to determine the category membership of an event or object, that attribute is criterial for the categorization. In other words, that value is what a referent must have to belong to that category; it is the attribute that experience has shown to be invariably present. Experimental studies demonstrate that individuals abstract the recurrent features or attributes (while they ignore or overlook the nonessential variations) and then generalize them to all other objects or events that contain these features when developing categories or meanings. Also, these studies reveal that a considerable part of our category system operates below the level of accessibility; thus, often we do not know why we get the meaning we do.[65]

An attribute is not criterial if it can be changed in value without having an effect on categorizing judgments; its presence should not detract from the criterial attributes when we are categorizing. Although noncriterial attributes (if recognized as such) do not determine assignment to a category, they are part of the meaning evoked when we hear the name of the category. Failure to distinguish between criterial and noncriterial attributes can result in the incorrect assignment of meaning. For example, if we think that the noncriterial attribute *dishonest* is criterial when assigning meaning to *politician,* our assignment of the stimulus to a category will be greatly affected. This problem is a common "block" to listening.

In our system of categories, there are four kinds: single attribute, disjunctive, relational, and conjunctive. The memory system has thousands of categories of each of these four kinds.

An example of a single attribute category is the category named *birds* because birds have only one criterial or essential attribute that distinguishes them from other mammals: this essential attribute is feathers. Indeed, birds have other attributes, but these other attributes are nonessential. Many of us may think that having wings that support flight is an essential attribute of birds; however, this attribute is neither universal among birds nor confined to birds. Some birds—such as ostriches and kiwis—cannot fly, and some animals that can fly—such as bats and bees—are not birds.

The second kind of category, the disjunctive category, consists of any referent that has any one of two or more essential attributes. To illustrate the disjunctive category, let us use the category named *out* as it applies to baseball. Among the many ways that a baseball player can make an out are the following: he may strike out, fly out, run out of the baseline when his purpose is *not* to avoid interfering with a defensive player, bunt the ball foul on a third strike, interfere with the catcher when there are less than two outs and a teammate is on third base, ground out if a defensive player reaches first base before he does, be tagged out when he is caught stealing, or be hit by a batted ball as he is running the bases. If you are knowledgeable about baseball, you no doubt can think of additional attributes that are essential to this category named *out*. However, we believe that we have listed a sufficient number of essential attributes to illustrate that a baseball player would be called out if he were the source or the receiver of any of the many essential attributes that constitute an out.

To illustrate the relational category, let us use the category named *quadrilateral*. A quadrilateral is a relational category because its essential attributes are relational or interrelated: there are four sides, and there are four angles. Without these features, a figure would not be a quadrilateral. We know that the square, rectangle, and rhombus are members of the general category named *quadrilateral* because these figures have this category's essential relational attributes. On the other hand, we know that an octagon does not belong to the quadrilateral category because an octagon's essential attributes are different from the essential attributes of a quadrilateral. Thus, the category named *octagon* is a distinct relational category whose essential attributes are these: there are eight sides, and there are eight angles. These examples, indeed, illustrate that a referent belongs to the relational category when there is a definite relationship between or among the referent's parts.

Into the final kind of category, the conjunctive category, we assign a referent that often requires our making a value judgment. A referent belonging to this category has no set number of essential attributes; however, the referent must have a sufficient number of essential attributes. What is a sufficient number? There is no fixed number. The number of essential attributes depends upon the judgment of the person who is assigning meaning to the referent. For example, if we were to ask you to define a leader, each of you would assign the category named *leader* to the conjunctive category and then make a value judgment regarding what the essential attributes of a leader are. One of you may believe that there are four essential attributes: trustworthiness, expertness, self-control, and sensitivity. Another may believe that, in addition to the four attributes just listed, a leader should possess impartiality and forcefulness. Still another may believe there are only two essential attributes: charisma and determination. If former President Harry S. Truman were alive today, he might list only one essential attribute: feistiness. After you have finished reading this book, we trust that each of you will include the desire and ability to listen effectively as an essential attribute of a leader. Hopefully, this one example of a referent belonging to the conjunctive category has illustrated that a referent in this category is often the source of misunderstanding when we are assigning meaning. Misunderstanding may result because each of us makes a personal judgment regarding what the referent's essential attributes are and whether the referent has a sufficient number of these attributes.

The complexity of the system of categorization can be shown further by noting that attributes are of two sorts and that categories are arranged in hierarchies. There are two sorts of attributes: formal (referring to the form and structure of the referent, such as the size, shape, and weight of various knives—butcher, kitchen, pocket, and hunting) and functional (referring to the use of the referent, such as the tasks various knives perform—slice, peel, file, and kill). For example, a power mower is a part of a larger hierarchy called *mowers* as well as a part of a larger hierarchy called *tools.* Thus, every referent in the universe is susceptible to multiple categorization since it can usually be assigned to several different formal and functional hierarchies. As a result of the complexity of categories, a single referent is often meaningless until a subcategory is specified by qualifiers (modifiers). Therefore, if a communicator wishes to successfully communicate, he or she must be specific in the words or sounds he or she transmits, and the listener must make every attempt to receive and attend to each stimulus since meaning is assigned according to the category or subcategory evoked.[66]

We establish most of our categories by actual or vicarious experiences. Therefore, each person's categories are different. When we first experience a new object or event, we begin to establish such a category. We learn the criterial and noncriterial attributes of the aural stimulus, assign it to one of four kinds of categories, and then assign meaning to it. After a category has been established, any other stimulus that we believe has the same criterial attributes—common features that we first abstract and then generalize from—is assigned to that category. The meaning that is evoked by the category or subcategory in which the stimulus is placed is then assigned to the stimulus.[67]

How categories are used when we listen can be illustrated in the following manner. In oral communication, we generally listen to several names such as are in this sentence: The steel-headed, forked hammer cracked. The word, *hammer* (a form-class word), is a general category that has its own criterial and noncriterial attributes. *The, steel-headed,* and *forked* are modifying names that summon forth subcategories of a general category, *hammer.* When we are assigning meaning, we cannot do so until we search our memory and find the category into which the stimulus "fits," and the brain makes only one search for category assignment at a time. In this specific example, one subcategory (the sum of the attributes of the four words) is evoked by the entire phrase: *The steel-headed, forked hammer;* the meaning—claw hammer—is then assigned. A second general category, *cracked,* is evoked by the action word. We then assign a complete meaning to the sentence. From this example, we can see that if we as listeners miss one word, for example, *forked,* we would assign the wrong meaning— riveting hammer, boilermaker's hammer, bricklayer's hammer, ball peen hammer, prospecting hammer, blacksmith's hammer, or cross peen hammer—as a result of our incorrect categorization. In this example, it is assumed that we have a category for claw hammer. However, if we do not have a category for a given stimulus (as in the case when we hear a new word or a strange sound), we can only guess at its meaning. Thus, we can very easily make an incorrect match; we cannot really understand if we do not know the category in which the stimulus "fits."

Incorrect Categorization. There are many reasons why incorrect categorization frequently occurs. The major reason is that each person has a different category system. Other common causes of listeners not assigning the meaning intended by the message source are the listeners' limited knowledge, narrow experiences, inadequate vocabularies, and rigidity in category assignment. Fortunately, as listeners increase their knowledge, broaden their experiences, enlarge their vocabularies, and temper their stubbornness, errors in categorization can be minimized. As listeners, we must demonstrate flexibility in recategorizing stimuli if we sincerely desire to assign more reliable meanings to the stimuli to which we attend.

Still another prevalent reason for listeners not assigning the meaning that the sender intended is that the message may arouse strong emotions in the listeners, and, as a result, the listeners may attach very personal and highly emotional meanings to the message. Suppose, for example, that a sender laughingly boasts, "When I left that bar last night, I was so drunk that I don't even remember driving home." Also, suppose that the listener—not known very well by the sender—had recently lost a niece in a fatal car accident caused by a drunken driver. The listener, after receiving and attending to both the vocal and verbal stimuli, searches through his or her memory until he or she finds the categories and subcategories into which the stimuli fit. Due to the listener's past experiences and highly emotional present feelings, the listener's assigned meaning (especially for the words *drunk* and *driving* and the laughing tone of voice) is quite different than the sender's intended meaning. Thus, when we are emotionally involved, we find that the assignment of meaning is an even more personal, complex process.

Up to this point, we have reduced the number of listening components included in the previously cited definitions to three: *receiving* (which includes hearing and

apprehending); *attending to* (which includes concentrating, receiving, and selecting); and *assigning meaning* (which includes analyzing, understanding, registering, interpreting, relating to past experiences and future expectancies,
engaging in further mental activity, assimilating, converting meaning to the
mind, receiving, identifying, recognizing, and comprehending). We have not,
however, resolved whether or not two other initially presented components should
be included in the listening process.

Remembering and Responding. It is our belief that remembering—the process of storing stimuli in the mind for the purpose of recalling them later—is
probably involved in all aspects of listening. Its importance, first, can be seen as
it relates to the holding of accumulated sound while we are initially receiving
and attending to a message.[68] Also, it is relevant to the act of attending to, since,
in general, only those stimuli to which we attend reach the LTM. Too, as we
categorize input data, we must search our memory bank for a "fit" in order to
assign meaning. Since remembering as it relates to listening has been discussed
under the listening components of receiving, attending to, and assigning meaning,
we do not feel that remembering should be included as a separate component of
the listening process; its inclusion would only be repetitious. Although we do not
limit the symbols involved in listening to verbal sounds only, we do agree with
Lundsteen's view regarding where the process of listening ends: "The term listening is appropriate when the person reaches the part in the series of steps where
his experience brings meaning to verbal symbols."[69]

In analyzing responding (also referred to as reacting), we think it is critical
to determine whether overt or covert response is meant. If covert response is
meant, the response could be a part of (1) the receiving process as our auditory
and sensory mechanisms respond to the original stimulus, (2) the attention process since the very act of attending to the stimulus is a response by the system,
or (3) the assignment of meaning process when we respond by categorizing the
stimulus so that it "matches" the intended meaning of the source. However, if
overt response is indicated, we do not consider responding to be a part of the
listening process. When listeners overtly respond, they are no longer listeners;
instead, they become the senders in the communication process. Weaver illustrates that responding is beyond the listening process:

> Let us assume that the single word "come" is a command. Whether you obey it or
> not does not concern the process of listening. You have "heard" it, which means you
> have received and attended to the data. The listening process concerns only the
> selecting of such stimulus data in order to "receive" it and the cognitive structuring
> of it.[70]

In his statement, Weaver also has called attention to a frequently held view
that we, too, feel needs to be clarified. Briefly mentioned in chapter 1, this view
is that many people think listening means agreement. We often hear a person
say, "Steve just refuses to listen to anything I say." A sender often makes this

type of statement because the listener does not agree with the content of the sender's message. This disagreement does not mean that the listener did not listen; the listener just did not agree. We wish to emphasize that listening does not necessarily mean agreement.

Additional Characteristics of Listening

Three additional listening characteristics that are mentioned in the definitions cited at the beginning of this section have not yet been treated. These qualities are that listening is creative, is purposeful, and is a process.

Creative Listening. Although Hook used the term *creative listening* to stress that "mental response is essential,"[71] listening scholars currently view the creative aspect of listening in a different light. They recognize that as listeners we each bring to the listening situation our own knowledge, experiences, attitudes, beliefs, mental set, category attributes, biases, personality, language, perceptions, and everything else that makes each of us a unique individual. Because each of us is unique and each of us develops our concepts personally, concepts can never mean the same for two individuals. We each can give only that which we possess, and when assigning meaning, we must—in a creative way—apply that which we bring with us to that which we receive and attend to. The creative aspect of listening can be observed when several people listen to one message and get several different meanings.

Purposeful Listening. Is listening purposeful? It is generally believed that there are purposes for listening.[72] The most commonly stated purposes are to appreciate, to evaluate, and to comprehend. Other purposes—also similar to those for reading, the other receptive language skill—are to associate or classify, to organize or synthesize, and to engage in problem solving.[73] Still others, as cited by the Commission on the English Curriculum of the National Council of Teachers of English, are to stimulate thinking, to respond to the challenge of new ideas and interests, to bolster a point of view already held, and to increase one's power to use language effectively.[74] Recognizing that there are many purposes for listening and that a listener cannot hold all listening purposes at once, we recommend that the listener consciously determine the purpose most suitable for the listening occasion during the early stages of each communicative act.

Dynamic Listening. The last characteristic that has been cited in several of the former definitions, including the six most recent definitions, is that listening is a process. We, too, believe that listening is an ongoing, dynamic process—a process involving three separate but interrelated processes (receiving, attending, and assigning meaning), all of which occur nearly simultaneously and yield a particular end result—listening.

Wolvin-Coakley Structural Definition and Model of Listening

This chapter has illustrated that the complex term *listening* cannot be adequately defined in one sentence. A thorough understanding of the processes involved in listening necessitates a detailed explanation. And, only after this understanding

Figure 3.3.
Wolvin-Coakley Model of the Listening
Process.
Drawing by Ted Metzger, Visual Technics.

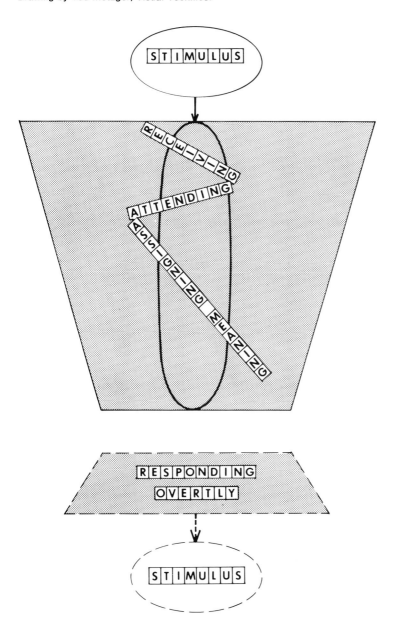

has been acquired can a definition of listening, stated in one sentence, be meaningful. Having carefully analyzed existing definitions in view of past and current listening research and having searchingly explored our own understanding of the listening act, we have chosen to define listening as *the process of receiving, attending to, and assigning meaning to aural stimuli.* For the purpose of this text, this structural definition of listening will be used. Our definition of the listening process might be depicted as a sequential process model (fig. 3.3).

This model is designed to illustrate the process of listening, the decoding of the stimulus through the auditory and visual senses. As you study the model, keep in mind that, throughout the listening process, our listening is enhanced or diminished by the efficiency of the sensory system and by the listening objectives which we set for ourselves.

The first aspect you should note in the model is that it contains two separate conical-shaped parts, the listening cone (the upper cone) and the feedback cone (the lower cone). The listening cone is wider at the top and more narrow at the bottom to exemplify that a given stimulus (aural or visual) can be interpreted in as many ways as there are listeners; and, since the assignment of meaning is a very personal matter, an individual will limit the meaning to "fit" his or her own system of categories. The feedback cone, on the other hand, is more narrow at the top and wider at the bottom to exemplify that if a listener chooses to respond overtly, the listener—who then becomes the source—draws on his or her personal system of categories to encode the message and sends a stimulus that is open to varied interpretations by various listeners.

Secondly, you should observe that the listening cone contains three components that we consider integral to listening—receiving, attending, and assigning meaning. To portray the intricate interaction of these three separate but interrelated processes, we have overlapped the components.

Another aspect you should notice is that a cylinder runs through the core of the listening cone. This cylinder represents the processes of remembering and covertly responding. Listeners remember the stimulus as they "run" it through the three listening processes, and they probably covertly respond to the stimulus as they "use" it while they are decoding the stimulus.

When studying the feedback (or overt response) cone, you should note that broken lines outline the cone and surround the stimulus. The broken lines illustrate that the process of overtly responding may or may not occur when listeners engage in the listening process. The stimulus exemplifies that an overt response is a second message. If listeners do send feedback, they become the sources of the feedback messages and create a different stimulus in the process.

The last aspect you should observe is the dotted lines that run diagonally throughout both cones. These dotted lines represent the perceptual filters through which listeners operate while they are decoding and sources operate while they are encoding. Additionally, the dotted lines serve to emphasize that the total communication process is a very personal and complex process.

Summary

In this chapter, we have presented a detailed description of what listening is currently believed to be. First, we have cited studies that provide experimental evidence that listening is a distinct activity. Secondly, we have traced the evolution of a listening definition from 1925 to the present. Thirdly, we have critically questioned and examined—in light of past and current research findings and theories—sixteen definitions of listening and four definitions of auding in order to determine what stimuli, what components, and what characteristics are involved in the listening act. Lastly, we have presented our structural definition—and a sequential process model—of listening: *Listening is the process of receiving, attending to, and assigning meaning to aural stimuli.*

Activities to Try

1. Before reading the chapter section entitled "A Definition of Listening," answer all questions (except number one) that are posed after the presentation of definitions. With the class, discuss your views on what the process of listening entails.
2. List the characteristics of a good definition. Then, evaluate the strengths and weaknesses of the cited listening and auding definitions (including the definition presented by us). Also, determine which of the cited definitions is the strongest.
3. List ten sounds that you hear in a normal day. Then, rank order the sounds according to the amount of auditory fatigue each sound causes you.
4. Identify five words that you have acquired through unique personal experiences and, as a result of these experiences, have specialized meanings for the words. Some of these words can be shared with the class.[75]
5. Identify five words that evoke highly emotional feelings in you and analyze what personal experiences have influenced these reactions. Some of these words can be shared with the class.
6. List three words whose once empty categories have become meaningfully filled since this course began. Some of these words can be shared with the class.
7. Discuss at least five purposes for which you have listened during the past five days.
8. Create your own definition and model of the listening act. All definitions and models should be mimeographed, shared with the class, and carefully analyzed and evaluated by the student and instructor.
9. Throughout the semester, you should keep a journal of your listening experiences. Each day, you should record one or more listening experiences in "diary" fashion. The following format may be most helpful:

Date:

Type of Listening (Appreciative, Discriminative, etc.):
(We recognize that you will not have these labels until you have covered chapters 4 through 8. For the time being, leave this section blank and plan to go back—at a later date—and label the types of listening you have done.)

Description of the Listening Event:

Your Response As a Listener:

What You Learned about Your Listening:

Work to get a variety of experiences in the various types of listening. Avoid recording just experiences you have at work, etc., but rather attend some events you might otherwise never attend so that you can broaden your listening skills as you do this journal. At the end of the semester, submit your journal to your instructor.

The following are examples of possible journal entries:

September 18

Therapeutic Listening

Today I listened as a friend described the options available to her family about her mother's illness. Her mother has terminal brain cancer and recently underwent an unsuccessful operation and radiation therapy. The decision must be made as to whether to have her undergo another operation or to leave things as they are and let the woman die in peace.

I served as a sounding board, offering no advice, but trying to give comfort and support. She finally decided to leave things as they are. I'm sure that her opportunity to talk through the situation with me was helpful.

I know people can solve their own problems, but I certainly realize how important it is to have that other person as a "sounding board" to articulate your thoughts and come up with a solution. If only more people would listen to others. . . .

October 10

Appreciative Listening

Tonight I went to the Kennedy Center Concert Hall to see Al Jarreau. The warm-up act was Dave Valentine. His violinist did incredible things with the violin! Then Al Jarreau came on. The man's voice is an instrument in itself. I realized that parts of his album that I thought were instrumental were actually his voice. The drummer would beat, and he would copy the sound to the exact pitch.

It was a very sensual experience. I wonder why certain music has such power. I love music and have learned how to avoid picking it apart but, instead, just letting it "happen" to me at a concert such as this one. It's a wonderful way to appreciate an artist's work.

October 29

Critical Listening

Today I listened to the 90-minute presidential debate. Ronald Reagan proved to be true to form. After listening to him talk, I trusted him even less than I had before the debate. I thought that he used his acting techniques (expressing surprise, disbelief, etc.) to win points. I found this approach to be very distasteful. The man who will be in that office for the next four years should be a sincere person, and that sincerity should be apparent with no necessary tricks.

Jimmy Carter impressed me more because he said what I knew in 1976—that there is no simple answer to complex questions. Reagan turned me off completely with his ready cure for all the "ills of the country." Also, when Carter challenged statements that Reagan was known to have made, Reagan said that he had been misinterpreted, which was definitely not true.

Also, I noticed that quite often in Reagan's answers and sometimes in Carter's responses, the point got lost. What made me very angry was Ronald Reagan using the example of talking to black youths and being sympathetic to our plights or situation, when I know full well that he's not going to be very helpful.

I guess I get too emotional when it comes to black issues, and I certainly need to work on controlling my emotions if I want to be truly objective in my evaluations.

November 28
Discriminative Listening

I talked to my brother yesterday, and he said that he thought my mother (who is a manic depressive personality) was going into a manic phase. He wanted me to call her in Ft. Lauderdale and see if I could tell. She has had this illness for at least five years, so by just listening to her talk, we can usually pick up on the warning signs. I called her this morning to check it out. I was listening for an increased pace in her speech, higher pitch in her voice, disjointed thoughts, and irrational thinking. After listening to her, I decided that she hadn't gone into this phase yet, but I could tell it was coming on. It's very important to detect it immediately so that adjustments can be made in her medication.

I am pleased that I've been able to sharpen my discriminative listening skills and deal with what could be an important medical situation. I wish more physicians and nurses could have this training!

Notes

1. John Caffrey, "Auding Ability at the Secondary Level," *Education* 75 (January 1955): 303–310; John Caffrey and T. W. Smith, "Preliminary Identification of Some Factors in the Davis-Eells Games," cited by Donald Spearritt, *Listening Comprehension—A Factorial Analysis* (Melbourne, Australia: G. W. Green and Sons, 1962), pp. 14–15; J. E. Karlin, "A Factorial Study of Auditory Function," *Psychometrika* 7 (December 1942): 251–279; Clair N. Hanley, "Factorial Analysis of Speech Perception," *Journal of Speech and Hearing Disorders* 21 (March 1956): 76–87.
2. Spearritt, *Listening Comprehension—A Factorial Analysis.*
3. *Ibid.,* pp. 21–22.
4. Carl H. Weaver, *Human Listening: Processes and Behavior* (Indianapolis: Bobbs-Merrill Company, 1972), p. 132.
5. W. Tucker, "Science of Listening," *19th Century* 97 (April 1925): 548.
6. Paul Tory Rankin, "The Measurement of the Ability to Understand Spoken Language" (Ph.D. dissertation, University of Michigan, 1926), *Dissertation Abstracts* 12 (1952): 847.
7. Julius N. Hook, *The Teaching of High School English* (New York: Ronald Press, 1950), p. 238.
8. Kenneth O. Johnson, "The Effect of Classroom Training upon Listening Comprehension," *Journal of Communication* 1 (May 1951): 58.

9. Walter Barbe and Robert Meyers, "Developing Listening Ability in Children," *Elementary English* 31 (February 1954): 82.

10. James I. Brown and G. Robert Carlsen, *Brown-Carlsen Listening Comprehension Test* (New York: Harcourt, Brace and World, 1955), p. 1.

11. Dana S. Still, "The Relationship between Listening Ability and High School Grades" (Ph.D. dissertation, University of Pittsburgh, 1955), p. 45.

12. M. S. Jones, "A Critical Review of Literature on Listening wih Special Emphasis on Theoretical Bases for Further Research in Listening" (M.A. thesis, North Carolina State College, 1956), p. 12.

13. Dominick A. Barbara, "On Listening—the Role of the Ear in Psychic Life," *Today's Speech* 5 (January 1957): 12.

14. Richard Hampleman, "Comparison of Listening and Reading Comprehension Ability of Fourth and Sixth Grade Pupils," *Elementary English* 35 (January 1958): 49.

15. Thomas R. Lewis, "Listening," *Review of Educational Research* 28 (April 1958): 89.

16. Charles Robert Petrie, Jr., "What Is Listening?" in *Listening: Readings*, ed. Sam Duker (New York: Scarecrow Press, 1966), p. 329.

17. Larry L. Barker, *Listening Behavior* (Englewood Cliffs, New Jersey: Prentice-Hall, 1971), p. 17.

18. Sara W. Lundsteen, *Listening: Its Impact on Reading and the Other Language Arts* (Illinois: NCTE/ERIC, 1971), p. 9.

19. Weaver, *Human Listening: Process and Behavior,* p. 12.

20. Robert O. Hirsch, *Listening: A Way to Process Information Aurally* (Dubuque, Iowa: Gorsuch Scarisbrick, Publishers, 1979), p. 1.

21. Donald P. Brown, "Teaching Aural English," *English Journal* 39 (March 1950): 128.

22. *Ibid.,* p. 130.

23. Donald P. Brown, "What Is the Basic Language Skill?" *ETC* 14 (Winter 1956–1957): 104.

24. John Caffrey, "Auding," *Review of Educational Research* 25 (April 1955): 121.

25. Edna Lue Furness, "Listening: A Case of Terminological Confusion," *Journal of Educational Psychology* 48 (December 1957): 481.

26. G. L. Horrworth, "Listening: A Facet of Oral Language," *Elementary English* 43 (December 1966): 857–858.

27. Lundsteen, *Listening: Its Impact on Reading and the Other Language Arts,* p. 9.

28. Weaver, *Human Listening: Processes and Behavior,* pp. 6–7.

29. Ray L. Birdwhistell, as cited in Mark L. Knapp, *Nonverbal Communication in Human Interaction,* 2nd ed. (New York: Holt, Rinehart and Winston, 1978), p. 30; Albert Mehrabian, *Silent Messages* (Belmont, California: Wadsworth Publishing Company, 1971), pp. 43–44; an interesting discussion of the functions of nonverbal cues is offered by Dale G. Leathers, *Nonverbal Communication Systems* (Boston: Allyn and Bacon, 1976).

30. For readings on the intricacies of visual discrimination, see Charles H. Graham, ed., *Vision and Visual Perception* (New York: John Wiley and Sons, 1965).

31. For a complete discussion of the physiology of hearing, see Hayes A. Newby, *Audiology* (New York: Appleton-Century-Crofts, 1972).

32. *Ibid.*

33. Table from Alexander Cohen, Joseph Anticaglia, and Herbert H. Jones, "Sociocusis—Hearing Loss from Non-Occupational Noise Exposure," *Sound and Vibration* (November 1970): 13. Reprinted by permission of the publisher.

34. For an update on EPA Noise Control Activity, see "Noise Control Program Progress to Date," Environmental Protection Agency, Office of Noise Abatement and Control, April 1979.

35. Daniel Rapoport, "Seattle: Laws, Residents' Attitudes Preserve Air of Tranquility," *The Washington Post* 5 November 1980, p. A–29.

36. Charles M. Solley and Gardner Murphy, *Development of the Perceptual World* (New York: Basic Books, 1960), p. 178.

37. Neville Moray, "Attention in Dichotic Listening: Affective Cues and the Influence of Instructions," *Quarterly Journal of Experimental Psychology* 11 (February 1959): 56–60; A. T. Welford, "Evidence of a Single-Channel Decision Mechanism Limiting Performance in a Serial Reaction Task," *Quarterly Journal of Experimental Psychology* 11 (November 1959): 193–210; Anne M. Treisman and G. Geffen, "Selective Attention and Cerebral Dominance in Perceiving and Responding to Speech Messages," *Quarterly Journal of Experimental Psychology* 20 (May 1968): 139–150; Neville Moray, *Listening and Attention* (Baltimore, Maryland: Penguin Books, 1969).

38. D. E. Broadbent, *Perception and Communication* (London: Pergamon Press, 1958); Neville Moray, *Attention: Selective Processes in Vision and Hearing* (London: Hutchinson Educational LTD, 1969), pp. 28–30.

39. J. A. Deutsch and D. Deutsch, "Attention: Some Theoretical Considerations," *Psychological Review* 70 (1968): 80, 84.

40. *Ibid.*, p. 84.

41. Moray, "Attention in Dichotic Listening: Affective Cues and the Influence of Instructions," pp. 56–60; I. Oswald, A. Taylor, and M. Treisman, "Discrimination Responses to Stimulation during Human Sleep," *Brain* 83 (1960): 440–453; C. E. Howarth and K. Ellis, "The Relative Intelligibility Threshold for One's Own Name Compared with Other Names," *Quarterly Journal of Experimental Psychology* 13 (November 1969): 236–239.

42. Anne M. Treisman, "Contextual Cues in Selective Listening," *Quarterly Journal of Experimental Psychology* 12 (November 1960): 246.

43. *Ibid.*, pp. 242–248; Moray, *Attention: Selective Processes in Vision and Hearing,* pp. 30–32; Moray, *Listening and Attention.*

44. Sir Frederic C. Bartlett, *Remembering* (Cambridge: Cambridge University Press, 1932), p. 190.

45. Weaver, *Human Listening: Processes and Behavior,* pp. 33, 37.

46. Magdalen D. Vernon "Perception, Attention, and Consciousness," in *Attention* ed. Paul Bakan (Princeton, New Jersey: D. Van Nostrand Company, 1966), pp. 37–57.

47. Broadbent, *Perception and Communication,* pp. 210–243; D. A. Norman, "Memory While Shadowing," *Quarterly Journal of Experimental Psychology* 21 (February 1969): 85–93; Tom Trabasso and Gordon H. Bower, *Attention in Learning: Theory and Research* (New York: John Wiley and Sons, 1968), pp. 212–221.

48. Arthur W. Melton, "Implications of Short-Term Memory for a General Theory of Memory," *Journal of Verbal Learning and Verbal Behavior* 2 (1963): 5.

49. Norman, "Memory While Shadowing," p. 93.
50. M. I. Posner, "Short Term Memory Systems in Human Information Processing," in *Attention and Performance,* ed. A. F. Sanders (Amsterdam: North-Holland Publishing Company, 1967), pp. 267–284.
51. *Ibid.,* p. 276.
52. M. Haider, "Neuropsychology of Attention, Expectation, and Vigilance," cited by Weaver, *Human Listening: Processes and Behavior,* p. 42.
53. Barker, *Listening Behavior,* p. 32.
54. Roger Brown, *Words and Things* (New York: Free Press of Glencoe, 1958), pp. 82–109.
55. R. C. Anderson, "Control of Student Mediating Processes during Verbal Learning and Instruction," *Review of Educational Research* 40 (June 1970): 349–369.
56. Lundsteen, *Listening: Its Impact on Reading and the Other Language Arts,* p. 37.
57. *Ibid.,* pp. 37–41.
58. Barker, *Listening Behavior,* p. 33.
59. Weaver, *Human Listening: Processes and Behavior,* pp. 42–59.
60. Jerome S. Bruner, Jacqueline J. Goodnow, and George A. Austin, *A Study of Thinking* (New York: John Wiley and Sons, 1956).
61. Roger Brown, *Words and Things.*
62. *Ibid.,* p. 206.
63. *Ibid.,* p. 14.
64. *Ibid.,* p. 10.
65. S. C. Fisher, "The Process of Generalizing Abstraction; and Its Product, the General Concept," *Psychological Monographs* 21 (1916): 1–213; C. L. Hull, "Quantitative Aspects of the Evolution of Concepts: An Experimental Study," *Psychological Monographs* 28 (1920): 1–86; Edna Heidbreder, "The Attainment of Concepts: III. The Process," *Journal of Psychology* 24 (1947): 93–138.
66. Weaver, *Human Listening: Processes and Behavior,* pp. 55–56.
67. *Ibid.,* p. 47.
68. Lundsteen, *Listening: Its Impact on Reading and the Other Language Arts,* p. 26.
69. *Ibid.,* p. 41.
70. Weaver, *Human Listening: Processes and Behavior,* p. 6.
71. Hook, *The Teaching of High School English,* p. 238.
72. Harlen M. Adams, "Learning to Be Discriminating Listeners," *English Journal* 36 (January 1947): 13–14; George Murphy, "We Also Learn by Listening," *Elementary English* 26 (March 1949): 127–128, 157; Barbe and Meyers, "Developing Listening Ability in Children," pp. 82–83; Donald E. Bird, "Listening," *NEA Journal* 49 (November 1960): 32; Ralph G. Nichols, "Listening Instruction in the Secondary School," in *Listening: Readings,* ed. Duker, p. 240; Barker, *Listening Behavior,* pp. 10–13.
73. Lundsteen, *Listening: Its Impact on Reading and the Other Language Arts,* pp. 32–33.
74. Commission on the English Curriculum of the National Council of Teachers of English, *The English Language Arts* (New York: Appleton-Century-Crofts, 1952), p. 334.
75. Robert O. Hirsch, *Listening: A Way To Process Information Aurally,* p. 17.

concepts you will encounter

Appreciation
Sensory Stimulation
Enjoyment
Aesthetic Experience
Music
Speech Style
Oral Reading
Theatre
Mass Media
Experience
Willingness
Attention

skIlls you should develop

Gaining Experience in
    Appreciative Listening
Developing a Willingness to Listen
    Appreciatively
Concentrating Attention

appreciative listening

4

Appreciative listening is the highly individualized process of listening in order to obtain sensory stimulation or enjoyment through the works and experiences of others. The process is highly individualized—perhaps even more individualized than other levels of listening—because it incorporates so many of a person's sensitivities in order to derive impressions and/or pleasure from the stimulus. As such, appreciative listening may represent basically an emotional response.

A person may listen appreciatively, for example, to a television movie. If the movie is a romantic comedy, the experience may be pleasurable. As a listener, then, the appreciation may be that of enjoyment. If the television movie is a horror story, on the other hand, the response may not be so pleasurable. The listener certainly will gain images and heightened emotions while feeling considerable tension at the horror depicted on the screen.

Variables Involved

Since appreciative listening is highly individualized, there are no criteria by which one can draw up a formula for the appreciation of anything for all people. However, we believe that an understanding of ours and others' views regarding appreciative listening will help you to develop your personal formula.

A clear controversy exists in many of the fine arts fields (art, music, dance, theatre) as to how to develop appreciation. Some scholars in these fields would encourage specific training in the components which make up the artistic expression (the elements of a symphony, for example). The stress here is on understanding the individual parts which make up the whole creative product. Others would suggest, however, that such specific training can interfere with true appreciation—that such training builds critical facility.

Paul Friedman, writing about training people as appreciative listeners, notes that listeners can recognize "subtle musical nuances that otherwise might go unnoticed" through knowledge of the composition of a musical piece.[1] Friedman recognizes, however, that overemphasis on understanding the intricacies of music may work against the appreciative listener: "If the listener becomes too concerned with the principles of musical form and structure, his or her enjoyment of the pure musical experiences may be diminished."[2]

It is not our purpose here to take sides in the controversy. We have known theatre people, for instance, who could not enjoy a theatre production because they were so trained to know every element of the production. Other theatre friends who have had similar backgrounds are able to set aside critical perspectives and truly appreciate a production. It would seem, therefore, that such differences reflect our point: appreciative listening is an individual process. What some may appreciate as listeners, others may not.

The individualized process of appreciative listening involves the interpreting of spoken, nonverbal, or musical language and the relating of that language to past experiences. A listener's perception, experience, background, mental set, and understanding all combine to guide his or her appreciative levels.

Opportunities for Appreciative Listening

Essentially, appreciative listening can include listening to music, the oral style of a speaker, environmental sounds, oral interpretation of literature, theatre, or radio, television, and film. It is not so much the source of the appreciative listening act as it is the individual response to it.

The appreciative listener listens for the power and beauty of well-chosen words or music which describe people, places, things, qualities, and abstractions. The color and mood of languages or music and the rhythm of language and music symbols are immeasurable except in an appreciative context. As the listener listens appreciatively to the reading of literature, or a theatre production, or a piece of music, or a speaker's rhetorical style, or environmental sounds, he or she will be listening to appreciate the works of others, to identify with their experiences, and to establish an emotional bond with them.

In order for listeners to develop this emotional bond when listening to music, music educators have stressed that our responses to music should fall in the fluid categories of sensual, emotional, and intellectual. Training in music appreciation is designed to unite these levels so that the listener can derive ultimate appreciation from the sound itself.

Machlis has identified the role of the appreciative listener in music:

> The enjoyment of music depends upon perceptive listening, and perceptive listening (like perceptive anything) is something that we achieve gradually, with practice and some effort. By acquiring a knowledge of the circumstances out of which a musical work issued, we prepare ourselves for its multiple meanings; we lay ourselves open to that exercise of mind and heart, sensibility and imagination that makes listening to music so unique an experience. But in the building up of our musical perceptions—that is, of our listening enjoyment—let us always remember that the ultimate wisdom resides neither in dates nor in facts. It is to be found in one place only—the sounds themselves.[3]

Another specialist in music appreciation, Charles Hoffer, suggests that there are three interrelated types of listening which can lead to enjoyment of music. One type of listening, "sensuous," refers to the physical effect of the music on the listener. A second type of listening involves the feeling or mood evoked by the music itself for the expressive meaning. The third type of music listening requires concentration of what happens in the music in order to appreciate the sounds and their manipulation.[4]

A more complex level of appreciative listening is listening to the oral style of a speaker. It is a difficult form of appreciative listening because, to be truly appreciative, the listener must filter out his or her responses to the speaker's content and concentrate on the speaker's rhetorical style. Jane Blankenship, in a popular book on speech style, has defined style as an individual's "characteristic way of using the resources of the English language."[5] These resources include the selection of words (word choice) and their combination (syntax) to achieve desired effects.

Several authors on speech style have characterized effective speech style. Wilson and Arnold provide us with one such set of characteristics which can be utilized as listening guidelines:

Accuracy—the precision by which ideas are expressed.

Clarity—ease of language.

Propriety—the appropriateness of the style to the speaker, the audience, and the occasion.

Economy—conciseness of language.

Force—vigor, power in language.

Striking quality—the vividness of the style.

Liveliness—the energy and movement of the language.[6]

These characteristics of style can be applied to the appreciation of the beauty and the power of the rhetorical language of effective public speakers. Contemporary speakers such as Martin Luther King, Jr., and John F. Kennedy were noted for their speech style. Consider the emotional impact of King's "I Have a Dream" speech presented in Washington, D.C., in August 1963, before a huge crowd at the Lincoln Memorial: "With this faith we will be able to work together, to pray together, to struggle together, to go to jail together, to stand up for freedom together, knowing that we will be free one day."[7] And we are all familiar with the emotional impact of Kennedy's conclusion to his January 1961, inaugural address: "And so, my fellow Americans: Ask not what your country can do for you—ask what you can do for your country. My fellow citizens of the world: Ask not what America will do for you, but what together we can do for the freedom of man."[8]

A unique appreciative listening experience is to listen to environmental sounds around us. A walk through a wooded parkland in the spring can provide the listener with a symphony of birds. The wind gently rustling the trees is another appreciative level provided by nature. Even the hectic pace of an urban environment can provide us with appreciative listening. And contemporary advocates of meditation reflect on the value of "listening" to silence.

We also create environments through sound. In the 1940s, media specialist Tony Schwartz developed a series of records believed to be the first to capture

Through listening appreciatively to the reading of oral literature, we can climb mountains, visit lions, touch stars. . . .
Photo by Robert Tocha.

sound that was part of everyday life. Known as the New York 19 project, the records enabled the listeners to experience actual sounds. Today, Schwartz (famous for his television "Daisy" commercial for Lyndon Johnson's presidential campaign against Barry Goldwater) argues that we create much of our environment through sounds—electronically mediated and amplified:

> This has radically affected the structure of sound for listeners and created a new relation between sound and space. Sound need no longer be contained within a physical environment that defines boundaries for the sound. Amplification of sound . . . is so overwhelming that it creates its own walls . . . that *contain* a listener.[9]

Listening to the oral interpretation of literature affords a further opportunity for appreciative listening. In the reading of literature, the reader serves to bring to life the author's material—prose, poetry, and drama—for the listener, providing sufficient interpretation to allow "mental pictures" to form in the mind of the listener. Oral interpretation can take several forms, from an individual reader presenting a program to the currently popular readers theatre medium.

An enterprising young man in Los Angeles, James McElvany, has marketed an ingenious oral interpretation project known as "Books on Tape." The firm rents out tape-recorded books to customers who listen to them on their automobile tape decks while commuting to work or traveling elsewhere. Customers in this million-dollar business listen to cassette-recorded current literary selections as well as classic adventures of Sherlock Holmes, James Thurber, Henry David Thoreau and others.[10]

Coger and White, in writing about the readers theatre medium, note that audience members can derive substantial benefits from their participation in the activity:

> For them, it provides the opportunity to explore the wide horizons of literature— great novels, memorable short stories, stirring poetry, and distinguished plays seldom produced in the theatre—and it challenges them to participate in the literary experience.[11]

In readers theatre, a group of interpreters presents the material to a live audience. While readers theatre depends on the interpreters to create the mental pictures, theatre as a medium provides yet another level of appreciative listening. The form differs from readers theatre in that it can be more explicit—scenery, lighting, costuming, and makeup combine with the actors to create an illusion for the listener.

Effective theatre calls on the listener to bring to play his or her imagination in creating the illusion. Recent theories of theatre have emphasized the need to involve the audiences as much as possible in the theatrical activity, viewing the listener as fifty percent of the total creative event. Consequently, much of the revolutionary theatre, for instance, is designed to elicit overt responses from the listeners. A recent Broadway production of *Candide* exemplifies this involvement: the orchestra and playing spaces were located throughout the audience areas, so the listeners were totally surrounded by the production.

On a different level, mass media offers appreciative listening through radio, television, and film. The listener's involvement in the medium has been theorized by Marshall McLuhan and Quentin Fiore. They suggest that the electronic media has shaped our lives, both personally and socially:

> Societies have always been shaped more by the nature of the media by which men communicate than by the content of the communication. The alphabet, for instance, is a technology that is absorbed by the very young child in a completely unconscious manner, by osmosis so to speak. Words and the meaning of words predispose the child to think and act automatically in certain ways. The alphabet and print technology fostered and encouraged a fragmenting process, a process of specialism and of detachment. Electric technology fosters and encourages unification and involvement. It is impossible to understand social and cultural changes without a knowledge of the workings of media.[12]

The popularity of the medium is obvious in this mass media society. While television and film are perennial favorites of the majority of Americans, radio may be making a "comeback" with a revival of popular radio dramas. At the University of Wisconsin, for instance, a series of radio plays, "EARPLAY," are produced for the Corporation for Public Broadcasting and distributed to the public radio stations of the National Public Radio Corporation. Radio stations in metropolitan centers are rerunning such popular series as "Stella Dallas," "The Great Gildersleeve," and "The Green Hornet." Cassette tape companies are distributing copies of many of the shows from the "Golden Age" of radio for persons who collect these broadcasts. Indeed, the famous Orson Welles's "The Shadow" broadcasts have repopularized the opening question, "Who knows what evil lurks in the hearts of men?"

The variety of media for appreciative listening provides the listener with a number of experiences from which he or she can choose. Despite the type of experience, it may be assumed that exposure to the stimulus, motivation, and attention enable the listener to gain from his or her experience what will be his or her own individual appreciation. From this appreciation, greater understanding and experience may result, providing the listener with a heightening of his or her appreciative capacities.

How to Improve Appreciative Listening

In this section, we will suggest and explain three ways the listener can improve his or her appreciative listening. However, let us first examine the suggestions that Barker, Hoffer, and Lewis and Nichols offer.

Larry Barker offers the listener five suggestions for improving appreciative listening in social or informal situations. He recommends that the listeners determine what they enjoy listening to most and then analyze why they enjoy these listening settings. Listeners are wise, then, to compare their likes and dislikes in listening with those of others and develop a strong sense of curiosity in approaching any appreciative listening setting. Further, Barker suggests, it is helpful to read and consult to learn more about the areas in which listeners do find enjoyment.[13]

Charles Hoffer, the specialist in music appreciation, recommends that the listener increase listening ability through (1) improving your memory for music; (2) concentrating on main themes and the important musical ideas; (3) hearing as much detail as possible; (4) encouraging your reactions to music; (5) avoiding the visualization of specific scenes; (6) applying knowledge to your listening; and (7) following a listening skills development program.[14] Ultimately, Hoffer suggests, the improvement of appreciative listening rests with the development of a positive attitude for creating an increased understanding: "Learning to listen is more accurately a matter of wanting to understand the music than it is of the techniques for understanding music."[15] This understanding, indeed, applies to the appreciation of all the art forms to which we attend as listeners. And through this appreciation we can expand and develop our experiences as human beings.

Thomas R. Lewis and Ralph G. Nichols have identified five steps that listeners can take to enhance the ability to listen appreciatively. These steps include the identification of the things we like most, the verification of why we like these things, and the observation of how these things we like most affect others.[16] In addition to dealing with the familiar things we like most, Lewis and Nichols recommend that we broaden our horizons in the search for new aesthetic expression. After the new aesthetic experience, it is helpful to study the art form, discuss it with others, and return to it for new insights.[17] "Appreciative listening, then, depends chiefly upon our willingness to learn."[18]

Gaining Experience in Appreciative Listening

The major step in improving one's appreciative listening abilities is to gain experience as an appreciative listener. The more practice you have in responding to appreciative material, either for pleasure or for impression, the more likely you will be to understand your responses and appreciate them.

It would seem to be helpful to gain experience in many different types of appreciative listening areas. The person who just attends rock music concerts, for instance, is deprived of the opportunity to respond to classical symphony concerts. A live theatre experience enthusiast could try opera or ballet productions. Broadening the range of appreciative listening can lead to the effect of understanding your responses and, perhaps, contrasting those responses with other forms. You may come to recognize why you prefer films over stage shows, for instance, and, consequently, establish firmer standards for your appreciative responses.

Developing a Willingness to Listen Appreciatively

In addition to gaining experience as an appreciative listener, it is useful to take advantage of the appreciative experiences and allow the material to elicit an aesthetic response from you as a listener. Friedman suggests that "simply being open to the impact that music can have on us, just allowing it to work its magic on our sensory organs, rather than analyzing its content or feelings, can be a major part of the listening response."[19] According to Charles Price, the listening response can be heightened when you are listening to an orchestra if you are willing to not "even listen to the orchestra, strange as that may seem to say. Listen, rather, to the music *through* the orchestra. . . . The musical play's the thing, not the actors. Any orchestra worth listening to should have this transparency about it."[20] Edgar Dale also calls attention to the importance of our being willing to listen appreciatively. Describing film appreciation, he emphasizes that appreciation is "to enjoy with understanding."[21] To understand, he argues, you must have a standard by which to measure the value of the experience: "Growth in appreciation comes through a willingness to try out the standards which others have found effective."[22] Your willingness to listen appreciatively— to let the material have the impact it is designed to have—can enhance your abilities as an appreciative listener.

Being willing to let the material work
its magic on us can enhance our
abilities as appreciative listeners.
Photo by Robert Tocha.

Concentrating Attention

In addition to gaining experience as an appreciative listener and developing a willingness to listen appreciatively, you can improve at this level of listening through careful attention to the aesthetic stimulus so that you can get the entire emotional impact of it. A person listening to the song of a cardinal or a mockingbird, for example, should concentrate his or her attention so as to appreciate the subtle nuances in the song. Machlis points out that true aesthetic listening requires more than the hearing of sounds: "To listen perceptively requires that we fasten our whole attention upon the sounds as they come floating through the air; that we observe the patterns' key form, and respond to the thought and feeling out of which those patterns have emerged."[23]

The broadening of your appreciative listening experiences can offer you the enrichment of expanding your aesthetic horizons and discovering new art forms. At the same time, it can help you discover new dimensions of yourself.

Summary

In this chapter, we have presented some ideas about appreciative listening—the highly individualized process of listening for sensory stimulation or enjoyment. This type of listening encompasses such experiences as listening to music, the oral style of a speaker, environmental sounds, oral interpretation of literature, theatre, television, film, and radio. Some appreciative listeners let the material "happen" to them, and, thus, they gain appreciation from the total sensory impact of the experience. Other appreciative listeners gain greater appreciation through information and even technical insight into the material and the presentation techniques. It is recommended that you gain experience as an appreciative listener, develop a willingness to listen appreciatively, and concentrate your attention to aesthetic stimuli in order to become more effective appreciative listeners.

Activities to Try

1. Attend a musical presentation (opera, concert, etc.). Listen attentively to the material. What sensory impressions did you get from the material? Did you enjoy the material? What factors combined to enhance your appreciation of it? Would you want to repeat the experience? What have you learned about your own appreciation of music from this experience?

2. Some early morning, go out into your neighborhood and listen to the environmental sounds around you. Do you hear city traffic sounds? Country/ woods' sounds? As you listen attentively, can you appreciate what you hear? Do the sounds create any poetic or musical images for you?

3. Attend an oral interpretation reading hour or a readers theatre performance. These presentations are designed to get you, the listener, totally involved through your own creative imagination. Did you visualize the scenes and the characters as you listened to the material? What did the readers do to enhance your involvement in the material?

4. Attend a theatre performance. Listen attentively to the material. What sensory impressions did you get from the material? Did you enjoy the material? What factors combined to enhance your appreciation of it? Would you want to repeat the experience? What have you learned about your own appreciation of theatre from this experience?

5. Some radio stations broadcast "reruns" of the old radio drama shows that were so popular ("The Shadow," for instance). If you can locate such a broadcast in your area, listen carefully to the presentation. What is done to enhance the material to create vivid images in the listeners' minds? Why do you think this type of presentation was so popular during the "Golden Age" of radio?

6. Attend a *new* appreciative listening event, something (a concert, a ballet, an opera, etc.) that you have not experienced before. Allow yourself to get involved in the material. After the event, reflect on your appreciation of it. Did you enjoy the experience? Why or why not? Would you like to repeat the experience? Would you like to learn more about this particular art form?

Notes

1. Paul G. Friedman, *Listening Processes: Attention, Understanding, Evaluation* (Washington, D.C.: National Education Association, 1978), p. 26.
2. *Ibid.*
3. Joseph Machlis, *The Enjoyment of Music* (New York: W. W. Norton and Company, Inc., 1957), p. 423.
4. Charles R. Hoffer, *A Concise Introduction to Music Listening* (Belmont, California: Wadsworth Publishing Company, 1974), pp. 10–11.
5. Jane Blankenship, *A Sense of Style: An Introduction to Style for the Public Speaker* (Belmont, California: Dickenson Publishing Company, 1968), p. 2.
6. John F. Wilson and Carroll C. Arnold, *Public Speaking As a Liberal Art* (Boston: Allyn and Bacon, Inc., 1974), pp. 215–225.
7. Martin Luther King, "I Have a Dream," reprinted in *Contemporary American Speeches,* eds. Wil A. Linkugel, R. R. Allen, and Richard L. Johannesen (Dubuque, Iowa: Kendall/Hunt Publishing Company, 1978), p. 365.
8. John F. Kennedy, "Inaugural Address," *Ibid.* p. 369.
9. Tony Schwartz, *The Responsive Chord* (New York: Anchor Books, 1974), p. 47.
10. Nancy Hoyt Belcher, "Heard Any Good Books Lately?" *Parade* June 24, 1979, p. 26.
11. Leslie Irene Coger and Melvin R. White, *Readers Theatre Handbook* (Glenview, Illinois: Scott, Foresman, 1967), p. 7.
12. From *The Medium Is the Massage* by Marshall McLuhan and Quentin Fiore. Co-ordinated by Jerome Agel. Copyright © 1967 by Bantam Books, Inc. Reprinted by permission of the publisher. All rights reserved.
13. Larry L. Barker, *Listening Behavior* (Englewood Cliffs, New Jersey: Prentice-Hall, Inc., 1971), pp. 81–82.
14. Hoffer, *A Concise Introduction to Music Listening,* pp. 11–12.
15. *Ibid.,* p. 10.
16. Thomas R. Lewis and Ralph G. Nichols, *Speaking and Listening* (Dubuque, Iowa: Wm. C. Brown Company Publishers, 1965), p. 192.
17. *Ibid.*
18. *Ibid.,* p. 193.
19. Friedman, *Listening Processes: Attention, Understanding, Evaluation,* p. 23.
20. Charles Price, "Listening to an Orchestra," *Southern World* 2 (December 1980): 36.
21. Edgar Dale, *How to Appreciate Motion Pictures* (New York: Arno Press, 1970), p. 6.
22. *Ibid.,* p. 7.
23. Machlis, *The Enjoyment of Music,* p. 3.

concepts you will encounter

Auditory Discrimination
Language Development
Phonology
Paralanguage
Sensitivity
Speech Patterns / Dialects
Visual Discrimination
Kinesics
Proxemics
Discrimination Preferences

skills you should develop

Refining Skills Included in Weaver
    and Rutherford's Hierarchy
Recognizing the Sound Structure
    of Our Language
Detecting and Isolating Vocal
    Cues
Understanding Dialectal
    Differences
Recognizing Environmental Sounds
Detecting and Isolating Nonverbal
    Cues

discriminative listening 5

The second purpose for listening is discriminative listening—listening to distinguish the aural stimuli. Depending upon the communication context, however, the stimuli also may be visual, such as a smile, a clenched fist, or a shrug of the shoulder.

Uses of Auditory Discrimination

Throughout our lives, we have relied heavily on our auditory discrimination ability. During our first few months, we began to develop this ability. We soon recognized the human voice, and we responded to it. Later, we turned our heads in search of the direction from which sounds were coming, and shortly thereafter we moved toward the sound sources. During our lolling stage, we listened to our own sounds and repeated them. Then, we began to imitate the sounds that made up our world—the sounds of family members, pets, and our environment. We were learning a language—a language consisting of coos, cries, happy tones, angry tones, loud noises, soft noises, close sounds, distant sounds, vowel sounds, consonant sounds, chirping sounds, perking sounds, continuous sounds, sporadic sounds, nonsensical sounds, sensible sounds, nasal tones, throaty tones, high-pitched sounds, low-pitched sounds, twangy sounds, and drawling sounds. As we grew older, we continued to enlarge our language of sounds and test our ability to discriminate among the varied sounds. Still today, we listen discriminatively, for example, to detect the arrival of a visitor, an elevator, or a rainstorm.

The Importance of Auditory Discrimination

The importance of auditory discrimination is documented in research on the language acquisition of children. It is generally agreed that the effective development of both our oral and reading vocabularies depends upon our auditory discrimination. One specialist in language development, Perkins, notes the role of auditory discrimination in the process of our oral language development:

> Long before his first true word is spoken, the infant has been working on his system for deciphering the mysterious stream of jabber he hears when people talk. The fact that he can recognize meaning of what is spoken before he himself can speak reveals

the ability to recognize at least gross differences in sounds on which meaning hinges before he can produce these differences. This ability is often called *auditory discrimination*. Less is known about how this capacity to recognize differences develops than about development of capacity to produce speech sounds.[1]

Ebel, summarizing the research on the development of reading skills, concludes that "the strength of many developmental reading programs appears to lie in their success in improving auditory discrimination of language sounds."[2] Thus, our auditory discrimination ability has played, and continues to play, an important role in the development of our listening, speaking, and reading effectiveness.

As adults, it is important that we possess highly developed auditory discrimination skills so that we can help others develop their discriminative ability. Many of us who are teachers, speech therapists, or parents especially need to develop our discriminative ability, for we are responsible for guiding a child's language acquisition. Only through careful auditory perception can we discriminate the child's language development (through, for example, *wabbit* and *yights* to *rabbit* and *lights*) and provide the necessary guidance.

As adults, we also need to develop our discriminative ability so that we can help ourselves become more efficient listeners. According to Fessenden, the first level of listening involves the isolation of the individual aspects of a message. This level does not include evaluation or analysis; it involves only "the recognition of the presence of specific, independent items."[3] Our proficiency in recognizing specific items strongly depends on our auditory discrimination ability, and without highly developed auditory discrimination skills, we cannot achieve our goal of becoming complete listeners.

Skills Involved in Auditory Discrimination

Developing our auditory discrimination skills is an ongoing process. When we are quite young, we begin to develop many of the essential auditory skills. As we grow older, we often need to refine those discriminative skills that are underdeveloped; also, we need to acquire and cultivate additional discriminative skills in order for us to master discriminative listening.

Refining Skills Included in Weaver and Rutherford's Hierarchy
A list of many of the auditory discriminative skills that we begin to develop early in our lives has been compiled by Weaver and Rutherford. After surveying the literature dealing with the development of discriminative as well as other listening skills, Weaver and Rutherford developed a hierarchy of auditory skills grouped according to the estimated time periods at which the various skills are generally developed. Although the authors of the hierarchy have distinguished between environmental skills (skills pertaining to sounds other than verbal sounds) and

discrimination skills (skills pertaining to verbal sounds), we will include both sections since both are relevant to the development of auditory discrimination:

Environmental Skills

Prenatal

Fetal movement in response to sound.

Infancy

Responds reflexively to sudden loud noises.
Responds to loud noises by crying.
Listens to the human voice.
Is quieted by sound.
Changes activity in response to the human voice.
Turns head in search of sound (VH*).[4]
Learns that people and objects make sound.
Learns that objects make sound with manipulation.
Localizes sound sources and moves toward them (VH*).

Preschool

Associates a sound with an object.
Repeats a sequence of sounds.
Learns that unseen objects make sounds.
Learns that sound sources can be labeled or named.
Given three noisemakers, can find the one that sounds different.
Can identify people and animals by sound.

Kindergarten–Grade 3

Learns that sounds differ in intensity (VH*).
Learns that sounds differ in pitch (VH*).
Learns that sounds differ in pattern.
Learns that sounds differ in duration (the length of time they can be heard).
Learns the concept distance in relation to sound localization and movement (VH).

Grade 4–Grade 6

Identifies sounds in the environment at certain times of day and evaluates them in terms of orientation and mobility (VH).
Promotes growth of echo perception and spatial orientation (VH).

Discrimination Skills

Infancy

Responds differentially to sounds.
Responds to his name.
Begins imitating speech sounds.

Preschool

Separates certain sounds from background sounds.
Identifies like sounds and different sounds.
Can match verbal sounds.

Learns that sounds differ in intensity (VH*).
Learns that sounds differ in pitch (VH*).
Learns that sounds differ in pattern.
Learns that sounds differ in duration.
Recognizes differences in word sounds.
Recognizes differences in initial consonants (cat-mat) auditorily.
Recognizes differences in final consonants (mat-map) auditorily.
Recognizes differences in medial sounds (map-mop) auditorily.
Recognizes discrete words within a sentence.
Recognizes sequence of words within a sentence.
Identifies accented words within a sentence.
Identifies number of syllables within a word.
Identifies accented syllable within a word.
Changes accent from one syllable to another.
Recognizes initial and final consonant sounds.
Recognizes short vowel sounds.
Recognizes long vowel sounds.
Recognizes rhyming words.
Recognizes and discriminates word endings (s, ing, er).
Discriminates temporal order of sounds within words.[5]

Although the skills listed here are concentrated at the lower educational levels, many of these skills can be further developed throughout a person's life. Developing our auditory discrimination skills, we repeat, is an ongoing process.

Numerous exercises can be devised to assist children in developing the auditory skills compiled by Weaver and Rutherford. For example, exercises—such as having children, with their eyes closed, (1) focus on sounds outside the room, inside the room, and within their bodies, (2) distinguish changes in cadence when they listen to the tapping of a pencil, and (3) determine differences in intensity of the clapping of hands—can help children develop three previously cited auditory skills. These skills are (1) spatial location—locating from where the sound is coming; (2) frequency spectra—determining how often sounds occur; and (3) loudness—determining the intensity of the sound that reaches the ear.[6] Exercises devised to assist children in developing other auditory skills listed in Weaver and Rutherford's hierarchy can likewise be beneficial.

Recognizing the Sound Structure of Our Language

A skill that we cultivate after our primary grade years is the skill of recognizing the sound structure of our language. If, for example, we are proficient in the previously cited skill of recognizing the various vowel and consonant sounds in the initial, medial, and final positions (a skill that we generally develop early in our schooling) and we know that English words do not begin with *sr*, we will not mishear *this rip* as *this srip*. Or, if we are trying to identify words at the beginning of a sentence, where they are quite unpredictable, and we know that *mg* cannot start a word in English, we will not perceive a sentence beginning with *I'm g* . . . as anything but *I'm* plus the start of a new word (whereas we could perceive a sentence beginning with *I'm a* as *I may* or the start of *I'm making*).[7] Research indicates that when we are categorizing stimuli, our initial decisions are made on a phonetic basis.[8] Therefore, if we wish to improve our discriminative listening and, thus, our assigning of meaning, we must increase our understanding of phonology (the structure of sound).

Detecting and Isolating Vocal Cues

Another skill that effective discriminative listeners must develop is detecting and isolating vocal cues—noting how a message is vocalized. Becoming efficient in this skill involves developing our sensory awareness to and increasing our understanding of paralanguage (vocal characteristics—pitch, volume, rate, and tone—and nonverbal vocalizations such as *ah*). We must be able to distinguish whether the paralanguage reinforces or contradicts the verbal message. When the paralanguage is contradictory, research shows that listeners rely more heavily on the vocal expression to infer the sender's feelings.[9] Mehrabian believes that a reasonably safe generalization regarding the impact of nonverbal communication, including vocal expression, can be made:

> When any nonverbal behavior contradicts speech, it is more likely to determine the total impact of the message . . . touching, positions (distance, forward lean, or eye contact), postures, gestures, as well as facial and vocal expressions, can all outweigh words and determine the feelings conveyed by a message.[10]

Mehrabian illustrates how this generalization may apply to a recorded message or a telephone conversation; if the vocal expression contradicts the verbal message, the vocal expression will determine the total impact. The impact will be negative if the words are positive and the vocal expression is negative, or the impact will be positive if the words are negative and the vocal expression is positive.[11] Thus, if we become more aware of vocal cues and learn to distinguish both the obvious and subtle differences in paralanguage, we may be better able to understand the messages of others, whether they be political candidates, job supervisors, or family members.

Understanding Dialectal Differences

On a less involved level, auditory discrimination can enhance listeners' sensitivity, particularly in their understanding of and their reactions to the speech of others. As listeners, we tend to stereotype speech patterns as a Southern drawl, a Midwestern twang, New York Brooklynese, "Havahd." In 1970, Dubin conducted a study that illustrates listeners' stereotyped reactions. He asked personnel interviewers in the Washington, D.C., area to react to tapes of speakers demonstrating the following dialects: general American white, general American black, light black, southern American white, and strong black. Predictably, the interviewers (who were not told what dialects they were listening to) more frequently selected the speaker with the standard white dialect for upper-level managerial positions and the speakers with the nonstandard dialects for lower-level positions.[12] Being aware of various regional and local dialects and understanding the differing dialectal characteristics through auditory discrimination can diminish the frequency with which we misunderstand words pronounced differently than we pronounce them as well as diminish our stereotyped reactions.

Recognizing Environmental Sounds

Likewise, sensitivity to environmental sounds through more careful discriminative listening can enhance our listening efficiency. Stories about the discriminative listening sensitivity which mothers develop to listen to their infants exemplify this level. One semester, some students of ours made a tape recording of fifty sounds ranging from the raising of a venetian blind, clicking pen, and perking coffee to a bellowing elephant in a zoo. Students at different grade levels in various urban, suburban, and rural schools were asked to identify the sounds. The results were interesting; they illustrated how nondiscriminative we can be. The researchers concluded that the problem is not so much that we are not exposed to a variety of sounds but that we do not attend, consciously, to the sounds.[13]

Measurements of Auditory Discrimination

A standardized measure of listening discrimination may be obtained through the utilization of the *Seashore Measure of Musical Talents*. This test provides separate measures for pitch, loudness, rhythm, time, timbre, and tonal memory. The tests have been used since 1919 as measures of musical aptitude, but they do provide indicators of our general auditory discrimination.[14]

Another test, the *Test of Non-Verbal Auditory Discrimination* (TENVAD), is patterned after the *Seashore Measure of Musical Talents*. This typed test consists of 50 pairs of tones in the same five subtests as the *Seashore* test. Each subtest has 10 pairs of tones that are the same or different in some way. Designed to be administered to groups of primary grade children who record their responses in test booklets, this test can be a useful tool for planning instructional programs in the primary grades.[15]

A third test that assesses the auditory discrimination of young children (ages 5 through 8) is *The Auditory Discrimination Test*. Two equated forms of the test measure a child's ability to distinguish between phonemes used in English speech.[16]

Visual Discrimination

Detecting and Isolating Nonverbal Cues

In face-to-face communication settings, the effective listener must also apply visual discrimination—distinguishing visual stimuli. These visual stimuli include nonverbal communication components (with the exception of vocal expression).

Our understanding of a sender's
message often depends on our ability
to "listen" with our eyes.
Photos by Robert Tocha.

Nonverbal communication represents what might be considered a parallel language. One aspect of this nonverbal language is kinesics, the study of body language, which includes facial expressions, bodily movements, postures, gestures, eye behavior. A second aspect is proxemics, the study of spatial relationships. These two visual aspects of nonverbal communication are important areas of research and analysis in the communication field.

They also are important to us as effective listeners; our eventual understanding of a sender's message often depends on our ability to initially distinguish nonverbal stimuli. Sociologist Erving Goffman stresses the importance of nonverbal behavior:

> When individuals come into one another's immediate presence in circumstances where no spoken communication is called for, they nonetheless inevitably engage one another in communication of a sort, for in all situations, significance is ascribed to certain matters that are not necessarily connected with particular verbal communi-

cations. These comprise bodily appearance and personal acts; dress, bearing, movement and positions, sound level, physical gestures such as waving and saluting, facial decorations, and broad emotional expressions.[17]

While an understanding of the principles of nonverbal communication can aid listeners in more discriminantly understanding their fellow communicators, we must be careful in applying the principles that writers frequently offer. Some of the popular treatments of the subject, while certainly increasing awareness of nonverbal communication, tend to overgeneralize and almost encourage listeners to stereotype the nonverbal message which is being sent. For example, Nierenberg and Calero, in their popular book, *How to Read a Person like a Book*, state the following:

> For centuries, man has put his hand to his chest to communicate loyalty, honesty, and devotion . . . women seldom use this gesture to communicate truthfulness, dedication, or loyalty . . . when a woman brings one or both hands to her breasts, it is usually a protective gesture indicating sudden shock or surprise.[18]

Despite the oversimplification inherent in attempting to interpret nonverbal codes, research does suggest that there are some nonverbal acts or events which can serve as perceivable stimuli for a listener. These stimuli can carry meaning to the listener only if, as in verbal communication, the intent of the stimuli and the code are shared by the two communicators.

Some research has been conducted on visual discrimination as it relates to receiver preferences for stimuli. Researchers have concluded that three factors may account for our preference for visual stimuli: the discriminability, the informative value, and the saliency of the stimulus itself.[19]

Our discrimination preferences may be tied up in our educational process. Research in reading indicates that most young learners prefer learning through listening in the early years. At about the age of twelve, the learner begins to prefer to learn information through reading rather than listening.[20]

Understanding our visual discrimination as it relates to auditory discrimination can help us to become more discerning in our reception of stimuli. McLuhan and Fiore noted our tendency not to trust the auditory input:

> Most people find it difficult to understand purely verbal concepts. They *suspect* the ear; they don't trust it. In general we feel more secure when things are *visible,* when we can "see for ourselves." We admonish children, for instance, to "believe only half of what they *see,* and nothing of what they *hear.*" All kinds of "shorthand" systems of notation have been developed to help us *see* what we *hear.*
>
> We employ visual and spatial metaphors for a great many everyday expressions. . . . We are so visually biased that we call our wisest men *vision*aries, or *seers!*[21]

This distrust of auditory input may have an effect on our discrimination of auditory stimuli. If, indeed, we prefer to receive information visually, that preference could lead us to more careful attention to and discrimination of visual communication codes. However, in spite of our preference, we must not disregard auditory communication codes.

Effective discriminatory listening, then, requires careful concentration, keen observation, and conscious recognition of the auditory and/or visual stimuli. Visual and auditory acuity—developed through motivation, sensory awareness, concentration, experience, practice, and care of the hearing and seeing mechanisms—can help us to listen with discrimination. There is so much in the world around us that we may be missing because we only see and hear it—we are not listening to it with any level of discrimination.

Summary

In this chapter, we have discussed discriminative listening—listening to distinguish the aural stimuli. First, we have noted the role that auditory discrimination plays in our listening effectiveness, language acquisition, and reading development. Also, we have presented a hierarchy of auditory discrimination skills that are developed during a child's early years—from infancy through grade six—and are strengthened throughout a person's life. Knowing this developmental sequence of discrimination skills and becoming adept in these skills can provide the adult with the tools necessary to assist a child in developing proficient auditory discrimination skills. Too, we have discussed additional discriminative skills that adults should possess: among these are recognizing the sound structure of our language, detecting and isolating vocal cues, becoming more sensitive to and understanding dialectal differences, and being more sensitive to environmental sounds. Lastly, we have stressed the importance of applying visual discrimination in face-to-face communication settings where an awareness and understanding of nonverbal communication can enhance the listener's understanding of a speaker's message. By developing and strengthening our discriminative listening skills, we can both broaden our world of sound and sight and improve our understanding of the messages of others.

Activities to Try

1. Prepare a list of twenty words; each list will consist of some words that are similar in sounds (such as yes, yet, gold, cold, low, blow, jaw, flaw, etc.). Participants will be paired and will sit back to back. One participant (the sender), stating each word only once, will clearly read his or her list while the partner (the listener) writes down what he or she hears. Then, the participants will exchange roles. There will be no feedback between partners. Participants may change partners as often as time permits. Before changing partners, each participant should score him- or herself by checking the sender's list. This practice helps listeners discriminate sounds and words.

2. Study the differences among the three major regional dialects (eastern, southern, and general American); these differences are discussed in the following texts: Wilhelmina G. Hedde, William N. Brigance, and Victor M. Powell, *Patterns in Communication* (Philadelphia: J. B. Lippincott Company, 1973), pp. 30–36, and Harlen Martin Adams and Thomas Clark Pollock, *Speak Up!.* (New York: Macmillan Company, 1964), pp. 434–436. Then, attempt to pronounce the following words as a native from Boston, Georgia, and Cleveland would pronounce them: there, laugh, court, car, better, board, Alaska, after, years, past, ask, path, answer, hot, four, house, high, class, and Florida. This practice helps you become more aware of and more sensitive to differing dialectal characteristics.
3. Participants will sit in a circle and close their eyes. Each participant will vocalize "oh" in a way as to express a different emotion. Participants will interpret the meaning of each "oh." This practice helps listeners become more sensitive to emotions expressed in vocal cues.

Notes

1. William H. Perkins, *Speech Pathology* (St. Louis: The C. V. Mosby Company, 1971), p. 115.
2. R. L. Ebel, ed., *Encyclopedia of Educational Research* (New York: MacMillan Company, 1969), p. 1083.
3. Seth Fessenden, "Levels of Listening—a Theory," *Education* 75 (January 1955): 34–35.
4. Discrepancies in the time when some skills are said to develop in sighted and visually handicapped persons are indicated by (VH*), and skills that apply only to the visually handicapped are indicated by (VH).
5. Susan W. Weaver and William L. Rutherford, "A Hierarchy of Listening Skills," *Elementary English* 51 (November/December 1974): 1148–1149. Reprinted with permission of the publisher.
6. Daniel Tutolo, "Attention: Necessary Aspect of Listening," *Language Arts* 56 (January 1979): 34–35.
7. Ronald A. Cole, "Navigating the Slippery Stream of Speech," *Psychology Today* 12 (April 1979): 78–79.
8. *Ibid.*, p. 80; George Mandler, "Words, Tests and Categories: An Experimental View of Organized Memory," in *Studies in Thought and Language*, ed. J. L. Cowan (Tucson, Arizona: University of Arizona Press, 1970), pp. 128–129.
9. Albert Mehrabian, *Silent Messages* (Belmont, California: Wadsworth Publishing Company, 1971), p. 56.
10. *Ibid.*, p. 45.
11. *Ibid.*, p. 43.
12. Harvey L. Dubin, "Standard and Non-Standard Phonological Patterns as Related to Employability" (M.A. thesis, University of Maryland—College Park, 1970), p. 51.
13. Larry Dobres and Cathy Gaffney, Discriminative Listening Project (University of Maryland—College Park, 1972).

14. Carl F. Seashore, Don Lewis, and Joseph G. Saeveit, *Seashore Measure of Musical Talents,* rev. ed. (New York: The Psychological Corporation, 1960).

15. Norman A. Buktenica, "Auditory Discrimination: A New Assessment Procedure," *Exceptional Children* 38 (November 1971): 237–240.

16. Joseph M. Wepman, *The Auditory Discrimination Test*, rev. ed. (Chicago, Illinois: Language Research Association, 1973).

17. Erving Goffman, *Behavior in Public Places* (New York: The Free Press of Glencoe, 1963), p. 33.

18. Gerald I. Nierenberg and Henry H. Calero, *How to Read a Person Like a Book* (New York: Pocket Books, 1973), pp. 125–126.

19. Cynthia R. Gilner et al., "A Developmental Investigation of Visual and Haptic Preferences for Shape and Texture," *Monographs of the Society for Research in Child Development* 24 (September 1969): 36.

20. See, for example, Donald D. Durrell, "Listening Comprehension Versus Reading Comprehension," *Journal of Reading* 12 (March 1969): 455–460.

21. From *The Medium Is the Massage* by Marshall McLuhan and Quentin Fiore. Coordinated by Jermone Agel. Copyright © 1967 by Bantam Books, Inc. Reprinted by permission of the publisher. All rights reserved.

concepts you will encounter

Comprehension
Understanding
Memory
Concentration
Vocabulary
Correlation Coefficient
Speech Speed/Thought Speed
Compressed Speech
Main Ideas
Transitions
Organizational Patterns
Details
Inferences
Notetaking
Outlining
Precis
Fact Versus Principle
Items in Sequence
Mnemonic Devices
Link Method
Oral Directions
Questions
Restatements

skills you should develop

Capitalizing on the Differential
    between Speech Speed and
    Thought Speed
Listening for Main Ideas
Listening for Significant Details
Drawing Justifiable Inferences
Being an Effective Notetaker
Recalling Items in a Sequence
Following Oral Directions
Formulating Meaningful Questions

comprehensive listening 6

The third purpose for listening goes beyond the discrimination of aural, and sometimes visual, stimuli to the understanding of the message. This listening for understanding is comprehensive listening. The comprehensive listener is successful if the message that he or she receives, attends to, and assigns meaning to is as close as possible to that which the sender intended. Remembering plays a major role in comprehensive listening when the listener's purpose is not only to understand the message being presented but also to retain it for future use.

Uses of Comprehensive Listening

In all phases of our lives, we listen to understand. Much of the educational process is based on comprehensive listening. We must carefully listen to lectures and class discussions in order to understand and retain an extensive amount of information. At work, we are often expected to learn new skills and new procedures through training programs which frequently utilize lecture and discussion methods for imparting knowledge. In our professional lives, we also listen to briefings, reports, seminars, conferences, oral papers, and other oral messages. In our personal lives, too, we listen to understand. We listen to our insurance agents explain our various policies, auto mechanics explain why our car is not operating properly, our accountant inform us of items that are now tax deductible, our children describe how their baseball game was won, our physician explain a diagnosis, media personalities share their views on current issues, and countless other people with informative messages. To be effective comprehensive listeners in each of these phases of our lives, we must concentrate on the message strictly for understanding, not for a critical judgment of it.

Variables Related to Comprehensive Listening

A careful reading of the research conducted in the field of listening shows us that of the five purposes for listening, comprehensive listening has received the most attention. A major reason why it has been studied so frequently is that it is the most "testable." A study which provides a pretest of information, a presentation of the information, and then a posttest covering the presented information can yield results from which we can make some generalizations about the listening comprehension of the persons in the study. While test results provide some clues regarding the listening efficiency of the comprehensive listener, such data also illustrate some of the many variables which tend to influence the listener's comprehensive ability.

Memory

One of the variables that are directly related to comprehensive listening is memory. Since we often measure comprehensive listening by a person's ability to remember the information that has been presented, memory is a significant variable in our listening to comprehend. According to Montgomery, an expert on memory training, we can greatly improve our ability to remember if we have a strong desire to improve our memory, concentrate on improving our memory, practice improving our memory, and care about people. Montgomery is convinced that we often do not recall names, for example, because "we don't really hear the names in the first place. We have no real desire to do so. We're lazy."[1] In a 1980 experimental study, Erickson, Chase, and Faloon investigated the effects of practice on the improvement of the short-term and long-term memory systems. Their findings suggest the following:

> . . . the reliable working capacity of short-term memory is about three or four units . . . and that it is not possible to increase the capacity of short-term memory with extended practice. Rather, increases in memory span are due to the use of mnemonic associations in long-term memory. With an appropriate mnemonic system and retrieval structure, there is seemingly no limit to improvement in memory skill with practice.[2]

It appears, then, that if we practice improving our long-term memory capacity, we can also improve our listening comprehension since memory is so closely related to comprehensive listening.

Concentration

Another significant variable to effectiveness in comprehensive listening is the person's ability to concentrate. Concentration on the message may be the most difficult task, particularly if the listener is not interested in the information being presented. To improve our ability to concentrate, we must develop mental discipline—determination not to rule out a message as "uninteresting" until we have searched the entire message for material that is relevant or helpful to us and determination not to allow external or internal distractions to prevent us from attending to the complete message, for concentration requires a concerted effort of will.

Vocabulary

Still another variable that appears to influence the listener's comprehensive ability is size of vocabulary. Although the precise relationship between listening and vocabulary has not been determined, "it can be concluded tentatively that size of listening vocabulary is probably an important variable in listening comprehension."[3] Since the assignment of meaning is an integral part of the listening process, we must have a sufficiently developed vocabulary so that we can expand our system of categorization and minimize our categorical errors. Only then can we assign more reliable meanings to the stimuli to which we attend. To increase our general vocabulary, we can read books containing advanced vocabulary levels, study vocabulary books and dictionaries, and take vocabulary building courses. Two recommended techniques for improving our listening vocabulary are (1) subjecting ourselves to a wide variety of listening experiences—especially experiences involving complex material that is more challenging than that to which we are generally accustomed—and (2) becoming more adept at determining word meanings from contextual clues.

Additional Variables
The relationships between listening and many other variables have been investigated by listening scholars; however, many factors have contributed to the delay of precise conclusions regarding the variables that influence listening comprehension. Among these contributing factors are (1) there has been a lack of scientifically controlled experiments, (2) there is not enough known about the validity and reliability of the listening tests utilized in the studies, and (3) much research has not been coordinated and collated. Although these factors have prevented "conclusive" results, the following additional variables currently appear to be slightly to moderately related to listening comprehension: *age* (with students gradually improving as they advance through school)[4]; *intelligence* (with the estimated correlation[5] being .46)[6]; *motivation* (with subjects—who had been forewarned that recall tests would follow the presentation of material, promised monetary rewards for listening and recalling, and mentally prepared by the anticipatory sets created by the experimenter—scoring significantly higher on listening tests than those subjects who had not been forewarned, promised rewards, or mentally prepared)[7]; *scholastic achievement* (with correlations ranging from .24 to .82)[8]; *speaking ability* (with correlations ranging from .36 to .79[9]; *reading comprehension* (with the average correlation estimated at being about .53 by Erickson and .59 by Duker)[10]; *verbal ability* (with correlations ranging from .37 to .76)[11]; *language and study skills* (with correlations ranging from .25 to .67)[12]; *organizational ability* (with correlations ranging from .36 to .53)[13]; *rate of presentation* (to be discussed later in this chapter); and *cultural status* (with correlations ranging from .33 to .48).[14] The relationships between listening and the following variables are presently less conclusive than the variables previously discussed: *sex, personality characteristics, interest in the subject matter discussed, auditory acuity, experience in listening, speech training, notetaking ability, visibility of the speaker, the speaker's use of gestures, speaker effectiveness, source credibility, difficulty of material, time of day, room temperature and ventilation, seating, position in family,* and *size of family.* As we can see,

additional research and more controlled research investigating the relationships between listening and these, as well as other, variables are greatly needed for us to better understand the variables involved in listening comprehension.

Skills Involved in Comprehensive Listening

Although we currently do not know all of the variables or all of the subskills involved in listening comprehension, scholars in the field of communication and related areas of study have provided us with several findings that, when put into practice, can enhance our listening comprehension.

Capitalizing on the Differential between Speech Speed and Thought Speed

Ralph G. Nichols, whose research in comprehensive listening pioneered the field, suggests that the efficient comprehensive listener should be careful not to waste the differential between speech speed and thought speed. As listeners, we can think about 500 words per minute while the normal speaking rate is about 125 to 150 words per minute. Thus, we may have close to 400 words of thinking time available to us each minute that we are listening.

Because we can think so much faster than speakers can speak, we tend to "tune in" and "tune out" during the message; while we are "tuning out," we are attending to other stimuli. We can imagine the danger here when some other stimulus becomes more attention getting than the message; we then stop concentrating on the message. The efficient comprehensive listener will be certain to "tune in" with regularity; instead of attending to external and/or internal stimuli, he or she will use the spare thinking time by mentally reviewing and summarizing what has been presented, weighing the evidence used, anticipating the speaker's next point, noting and assigning meaning to nonverbal messages being presented, and listening for what is not said. Nichols emphasizes the importance of our using our spare thinking time efficiently:

> Not capitalizing on thought speed is our greatest single handicap. The differential between thought speed and speech speed breeds false feelings of security and mental tangents. Yet, through listening training, this same differential can be readily converted into our greatest asset.[15]

A relatively new research technique may help the comprehensive listener reduce the time differential between speech speed and thought speed. Communication scholars have been studying the effects of compressed speech—speech that consists of increasing the word rate of a previously recorded message without essential alteration. The process was first done by having the speaker speak more rapidly. It was then accomplished by speeding up the recorder. Next, a cut-and-splice method was employed. Now, material can be compressed electronically. Until 1950, most scholars believed that "increasing rate led to a decrease in listening efficiency."[16]

Recently, however, researchers have demonstrated that (1) speed of speech can be effectively doubled without impairing intelligibility[17] and that (2) speaking rates can be increased with 50 percent compression without loss of comprehension.[18] The optimal speaking rate for comprehension appears to be between 275 and 300 words per minute.[19]

Since we do think much more rapidly than the normal conversational speech rate, it stands to reason that we can handle auditory input at a much faster rate; many recent studies have supported this view. Foulke, et al., studying the effect of compressed speech on the comprehension ability of 291 blind children, found that there was no significant loss of comprehension of messages recorded up to 275 words per minute.[20] It has also been found that sighted students benefit from using time compressed speech. In 1974, Short, using a Syracuse University population of 90 students, found that subjects who used variable speed compressors saved significant amounts of time (an average time savings of 32 percent) and scored significantly higher on posttests than those subjects who learned the same material at normal speed; additionally 70 percent of those who used variable speech adapted to it quickly and liked listening at faster than normal rates.[21]

Currently, compressed speech is being used in many segments of society—including business, education, and public services. In industry, it has been found to be a cost effective tool. In addition to providing its users with a time-saving means to review recorded dictation, check recorded meetings, reports, and telephone answering tapes, and compile taped inventory records, it has been found to improve the concentration and comprehension of new employees when it has been utilized in training programs. In the field of education, it has led to substantial savings in time. Instructors can preview auditory material faster, media specialists can review media seminar tapes in less time, and students—as they listen to taped lecture material—can decrease their review time while they increase their comprehension ability. Still another educational application of compressed speech is its use in tutorial programs. Rome—who originated the use of speech compressors in the autotutorial program at Western Connecticut State College—believes speech compressors possess a promising future:

> We can finally provide something effective for those students who do not learn best through the visual modality. With the introduction of lower cost rate-controlled recorders, we have a viable alternative for learning which may rival the printing press as a way of disseminating information.[22]

Law enforcement officers and hospital personnel, too, have found compressed speech useful. It can assist them in providing professional training, reviewing and previewing auditory data, checking logged calls and interviews, rapidly transferring information between shifts, and providing professional updating. The current use of compressed speech indicates that compressed speech offers widespread potential for application in improving the listening and learning of those involved in these as well as many other segments of society.[23]

It is likely that the use of compressed speech will soon extend beyond business, education, and public services to television advertising. National advertisers are presently testing the effectiveness of commercials compressed by a subtle 20 percent. Although 20 percent compression may not seem very significant to us, to advertisers it means cutting costs. If a 36-second commerical, for instance, were aired during the 1980 Winter Olympics, it would have cost $81,000. The same commercial, run in 30 seconds, would have saved the advertiser $13,500. An advertiser of the 1980 "Who Shot J. R.?" segment of *Dallas* would have saved even more—nearly $46,000—if the advertiser had compressed a 36-second commercial by 20 percent. Not only could advertisers save money if they compressed the rate of their commercials, but also they could increase the attention and retention of their listeners if researchers in the advertising field can further substantiate the research findings of LaBarbera, Shoaf, and MacLachlan—who found that subjects who listened to (and viewed) commercials increased in speed by 25 percent had higher levels of attentional effort and greater recall two days later than did subjects who listened to (and viewed) commercials played at their regular speed.[24]

Speech compressors or rate-controlled recorders are now readily available and fairly inexpensive, and they could offer you interesting demonstrations as to the possibilities of reducing time and improving listening comprehension. One speech controller is the VSC Speech Controller, also known as the Variable Speech Control tape recorder; weighing 4.3 pounds, this recorder is manufactured by the Variable Speech Control Corporation (VSC), and it can be purchased on a ten-day trial basis. In addition to including all of the features of a standard recorder, it has a slide lever (labeled VSC rate) graduated from 0.6 to 2.5. These numbers, indicating the amount of slowdown or speedup of the tape, allow the user to control the playback rate of any standard audio cassette without distortion of pitch or creation of a "chipmunk" or "Donald Duck" effect; that is, a tape originally recorded at 150 words per minute (wpm) could be played from 90 wpm (if the slide lever were placed at 0.6) up to and including 375 wpm (if the lever were placed at 2.5).[25] Another speech compressor, particularly designed for use by the blind but not limited to their use, is the AmBiChron Model 101, manufactured by AmBiChron. This battery-operated pitch corrector (weighing less than one pound) provides portable time compression and expansion. Model 101 maintains natural pitch over a playback speed range from less than one-half normal speed to above three times normal speed.[26] A third speech compressor is the Varispeed-II, manufactured by Lexicon Corporation; this cassette recorder has a playback time ranging from 200 percent to 40 percent of the original recording time.[27] Each of these compressors holds much promise for the individual who wishes to become a more efficient comprehensive listener.[28]

Despite the technological advances in compressed speech, however, its usefulness to the general listener remains limited. Just as speed readers have difficulty applying the speed-reading techniques to difficult technical material, "speed listeners" report little carry-over to complex listening situations.

Listening for Main Ideas

One important skill which can help to enhance our efficiency in using the speech speed-thought speed differential is knowing for what we should listen. Several scholars suggest that the efficient listener listens to get the main ideas from the message; he or she should concentrate primarily on the main points rather than on the supporting data. If you consider that we tend to be able to recall—at a later time—no more than 25 percent of what we listen to today, it makes sense that we should strive to concentrate on understanding the key concepts of a message rather than the details that exemplify the concepts.

There are several ways we can become more adept at identifying the main idea(s) of an oral message provided that the speaker clearly knows his or her purpose and direction. We must strive to identify the main idea of the entire message as well as the main concepts presented within the message. To help us identify the main idea of the entire message (known also as the central idea of thesis statement), we must become aware of the positions where most senders place the main idea. It may be stated in the title, stated shortly after the introduction has been presented, repeated throughout the speech (since senders often repeat important concepts), stated in the summary of the speech, or subtly implied (suggested) in the speech as a whole and recognized only after we have listened to the complete message. If the main idea is stated, we must learn to identify transitions that speakers use when they are introducing or discussing the main idea; some of these transitions are the following: "I want to make one impression on you, and that is . . ."; "Today, we are going to discuss . . ."; "Simply stated, the issue is . . ."; "Let us today examine why . . ."; "Today, we will be covering . . ."; "There are three methods that we . . ."; "Our subject this evening is . . ."; "And so we can conclude that . . ."; and "In conclusion, then, I want you to understand that . . ."

In addition to knowing where the main idea is often expressed and what transitions are frequently used to introduce a main idea, efficient listeners must also know what nonverbal behavioral changes speakers often use when they are stating a main idea. If we become skilled in listening to and watching for these changes in rate, volume, pitch, bodily movements, gestures, eye contact, and other nonverbal cues, we will be able to more readily identify the main idea of a message. Additionally, when we are identifying the main idea, we must exercise caution that we not make the main idea too broad (by including more than is in the message) or too narrow (by including only some concepts); we must be specific, yet comprehensive enough to include all of the relevant concepts that have been presented.

When identifying main concepts within a message (those concepts that are used to establish the main idea of a speech), we must be knowledgeable of many general organizational patterns. Among these patterns are the following:

Unfolding

Introduction
Statement of thesis sentence
Statement of first issue

Discussion of first issue
Statement of second issue
Discussion of second issue
Statement of third issue
Discussion of third issue, etc.
Conclusion

One-Issue

Introduction
Statement of thesis sentence
Example
Example
Example, etc.
Conclusion

Partitioning

Introduction
Statement of thesis sentence
Restatement of thesis and division
Statement of first issue
Discussion of first issue
Restatement of first issue
Statement of second issue
Discussion of second issue
Restatement of second issue
Statement of third issue
Discussion of third issue
Restatement of third issue, etc.
Conclusion—Summary[29]

Additionally, we must be aware of the previously mentioned nonverbal cues and numerous other transitions, such as "first," "along with," "not only . . . but also," "finally," "next in importance," "in addition to this," "on the other hand," "also," "following this step is," "a somewhat similar method is," "above all." If we train ourselves to listen primarily for main ideas/concepts, we will not become so preoccupied with facts and details that we lose the main ideas; we must be first idea listeners and then fact/detail listeners.

Listening for Significant Details

After we have become proficient in listening for main ideas, we should then develop the skill of listening for significant details that the speaker uses to support his or her main ideas. These details may be in the form of facts, examples, statistics, restatements, anecdotes, personal incidents, analogies, references to reliable sources, descriptions, contrasts, definitions. As we listen for significant details, we must again be aware of transitions that indicate that details are following. Some of these transitions are "for example," "to illustrate this point," "this can be seen by," "for instance," "by way of illustration," "that is," "to explain," "in other words," "comparable to," "the fact is," "on the contrary," "according to." By recognizing these transitional words, we can more readily identify supporting details. We must, however, distinguish between the supporting details that are relevant and those that are irrelevant to the main ideas that the speaker is presenting, and we must separate what we have learned in the past from what we are listening to now if we hope to be accurate in our listening. Identifying the main ideas and supporting details and understanding the inter-relationships between the ideas and details will aid us in assigning more reliable meanings to the sender's message.

Drawing Justifiable Inferences

Another skill that the comprehensive listener should develop is the ability to draw justifiable inferences. Inferences (implications) are data that are not stated but are implied. Efficient listeners must not only listen to what is explicitly stated but also listen for what is implicitly suggested. Because each listener draws his or her own inferences, they are very personal and subject to error. Weaver stresses the importance of making inferences and the difficulty of separating personal meanings and the speaker's meanings: "It is likely that the most important part of our communication is the part we infer. And yet we do this through our screen of personal biases, our needs, and our affective states."[30] The more we know about ourselves and our personal biases, needs, and emotions, the less likely we are to make errors in drawing inferences. The following steps will help us in drawing justifiable inferences:

1. Fully understand the stated ideas.
2. Reason by logical thinking to the inferred idea.
3. Determine the fairness or justice of the inferred idea.
4. Base reasoning on the idea stated by the sender; do not be misled by our personal opinions, feelings, biases, or "what seems reasonable" but is not stated by the communicator.

Let us illustrate how we can apply these four steps when we are listening. Suppose we hear a woman who is running for county executive make this statement about her opponent: "How can you think of voting for him? He didn't even attend his own mother's funeral!" Our first step is to understand fully the stated idea, which—in our example—is in the form of a question and a statement. The question is why or for what reason(s) are we thinking of voting for her opponent; the statement is that her opponent was not present at his mother's funeral. Once we fully understand the stated idea, we should then apply the second step— reason by logical thinking to the inferred idea. In our example, the woman running for office wants us to vote for her; she does not want us to vote for her opponent. She wants to give us a reason for not voting for him. She *hopes* that we will infer—from her stated idea—that if her opponent did not care enough about his own mother to attend her funeral, he certainly would not be responsive to the needs and concerns of us, most of whom are strangers. She *hopes* that if we draw the inference she wants us to draw, we will not want him to be our representative and, therefore, we will not vote for him.

Our next step is to determine if the inference we have drawn is justifiable or fair. We have drawn the inference that she had hoped we would, but we do not have to accept what she silently said. Is the critical issue regarding her opponent's qualifications for county executive whether or not he attended his mother's funeral? Regardless of our personal feelings concerning the manner in which a person should cope with the death of a family member, a person's presence or absence at the funeral of a family member should not be the critical issue upon which we base our voting preference. We do not know if, in fact, he did not attend his mother's funeral. Nor do we know why he was not present at the funeral—if he were not present. He could have been someplace where he could not have been reached, he could have been a prisoner of war or a hostage, or he could be a person who prefers remembering a loved one as she or he was in life rather than in death. If we carefully analyze the justification of each inference we draw—as we have carefully analyzed this one, we will become more efficient listeners. Hopefully, this example has helped you to understand how to apply the first three steps that assist listeners in drawing justifiable inferences.

Let us now illustrate how listeners can apply the fourth step—base our reasoning on the stated idea rather than on personal views. Suppose that we later hear the woman's opponent speak. In his speech, he makes the following statement: "I spent the first fifteen years of my life in the slums and on welfare, and now I'm running for county executive." He *hopes* that we will infer from this statement that he is a man who has overcome his poor beginnings and has become a strong, determined leader despite his early hardships; thus, he can help us overcome our problems. However, this time we are misled by our personal views, and our personal meanings lead us to draw these inferences: Here is a man who, having been on welfare himself, will raise our taxes in order to provide more revenue for welfare assistance programs; then, he will provide more handouts to all the lazy, no-good people in our country. Because we often allow our personal views to be the basis of our reasoning—as we did in this illustration, we frequently make errors when drawing inferences.

Being aware of these four steps and practicing them should assist us in drawing justifiable inferences when the speaker does not explicitly state his or her position, specific details, or relationships. And, such steps, then, can enhance our comprehension of the overall message.

Being an Effective Notetaker

Though few studies have correlated notetaking and efficient listening behavior, notetaking—when done properly—can be valuable to listener comprehension in many ways. One value is that notetaking can improve our ability to concentrate in lecture settings as well as in public listening situations. A second value is that notetaking can motivate us to take the initiative in putting the message content into our long-term memory systems. Still another value is that notetaking can "lock in print" information that we may need to refer to at a later time; shortly after we have taken our notes, we should review them, clarify them, add to them, and—if necessary—restructure them so that they will be more meaningful to us now as well as at a later time. Reviewing them will also aid us in retaining the information more permanently.

There are several points we should consider when we take notes. The first is that we should determine whether or not we need to take notes. Are we going to use immediately the material presented? Can we retain the information without taking notes? Do we have high concentration abilities? If the answer is yes to these questions, we probably do not need to take notes. If, however, we must retain the information for future reference, it is recommended that we take notes in a manner that will enhance rather than detract from our listening. Secondly, we should be physically, mentally, and psychologically prepared to take notes. Physically, we should have paper and pen ready, we should be sitting upright, and we should be giving our attention to the speaker. Mentally, we should, if possible, obtain—prior to the listening situation—background information on the topic and the speaker. Psychologically, we should have a positive, open-minded attitude toward the communicative situation. Also, we should not begin taking notes too soon after the speaker has begun his or her presentation. We should wait several minutes until we have determined the speaker's organizational pattern or his or her lack of an organizational pattern, and then we must adjust our notetaking style to the speaker's style of presentation; if we are to be good listeners, we must be flexible notetakers. When we do take notes, we must not take them in a mechanical fashion for the sole purpose of external storage; our task is not accomplished unless internal rehearsal of the message accompanies the act of notetaking. Lastly, we must determine what method of notetaking we should use, for there are several methods.

The most commonly used method of notetaking is probably the outlining method. The strengths of this system are that notes are neat, organized, easily filed, useful for review, and helpful in developing our ability to coordinate items of equal rank and subordinate items of less importance. There are, however, two major weaknesses to this system: the system is impractical if the speech does not follow some definite plan of organization (and less than one half of the speeches are carefully organized), and listeners often become so preoccupied with the symmetry and the mechanics (indentations, capitalizations, I, A, i, a, etc.) that they become confused and lose important concepts and supporting details of the message. Before we begin to outline our notes, we must listen for several minutes so that we can detect the speaker's structure; if the speaker's material is organized, then we may choose this method for our notetaking. However, if the speaker's material is unorganized, we must choose another method. Remember Nichols's advice: "There are few things more frustrating than to try to outline an unoutlinable speech."[31] When we do choose to outline our notes, we must be skilled in identifying the central ideas, noting the significant details, understanding interrelationships between ideas and details, recognizing what ideas are important and what ones are of little concern, recognizing transitional devices, and knowing well the mechanics of outlining.

Another method of notetaking is the précis method. When we use this system, we listen for several minutes, we mentally summarize what is being said, and then—at widely-spaced time intervals—we record a summary of what we have heard by writing a short paragraph or a one- or two-sentence abstract. We repeat these three steps until the message has been completed. The strengths of this system are that our notes are brief, easily filed, and useful for review; also, this system can be used for both organized and disorganized messages. One major weakness is that this system results in too much writing at one time. During the periods of writing, the speaker goes on, and the listeners are losing parts of the message. A second weakness is that significant details are often slighted or omitted. Still another weakness is that often we may not have time to write a complete précis; if we only have enough time to write down a key word or phrase, we must—as soon as possible after the speech—expand our notes so that they will be more meaningful to us when we review them later. If we use this method of notetaking, we must be skilled in recognizing the common structure of most concepts (with the speaker going from the main idea to supporting details—the deductive approach—or going from supporting details to the main idea—the inductive approach); recognizing transitional devices that are signals that a main point follows ("More important than . . . is . . . ," "Now that we have considered . . . , let's look at a second consideration," "Another main point is . . . ," etc.); knowing when to listen, when to mentally summarize, and when to write the abstract (at the ends of spoken units of thought); and knowing what to include in our précis (the thesis sentence, generalizations or main concepts, and the final appeal that the speaker makes).

A third method of notetaking is the fact versus principle method. When using this system, we divide our paper vertically in half. In the right-hand column, we list the important principles (main ideas); in the left-hand column, we list the important facts (verifiable supporting data) which we may need to recall later. If a question arises as we listen, we state it at the bottom of the appropriate column. The strengths of this system are that the notes are brief and easily filed; also, this system is especially workable for disorganized messages, it flows naturally as the speaker develops the message, and it provides a clear means for recalling key concepts as they were developed. The system also has weaknesses; often our understanding of the basic structure of the message is lost, and it is often difficult to distinguish between facts and principles. If we use this method of notetaking, we must be skilled in distinguishing between supporting data and main ideas, differentiating between relevant and irrelevant data, understanding interrelationships between man ideas and details, recognizing transitional devices, and noting a possible interrelationship among the principles. Additionally, it is crucial that shortly after the message has been completed, we structure our notes so that we can give order to the speaker's message (if it were disorganized).

Recalling Items in a Sequence

Another skill that listening scholars frequently recommend for proficiency in comprehensive listening is the ability to recall items in a sequence. As listeners, we often need to recall simple sequences when we are orally given phone numbers, route directions, shopping lists, names of new acquaintances, lists of tasks, dates of upcoming events, addresses, and numerous other data. A typical example of a situation in which listeners need to utilize this ability can be found in the most widely used listening test, the *Brown-Carlsen Listening Comprehension Test.* Brown and Carlsen include *immediate recall* as one of the five listening skills that their test measures. One of their test items in Form AM is the following: "In the statement, 'Send three boxtops with your name and address and 20 cents to Box 24, Denver 18, Colorado, to receive the special gift offer,' the *number of cents* to be enclosed is _____ ?"[32] As we look at this example and recall similar examples from our daily lives, we become aware of the importance of being able to recall items in a sequence. We know, as stressed in previous chapters, that if we are to develop this skill, we must attend to the stimuli so that they will reach our long-term memory system where they must be stored if we wish to recall them later.

A technique that may help us to remember data in sequential order is the utilization of mnemonic devices—memory aids that elaborate on the stimuli being attended to and help us commit the stimuli to the LTM. A mnemonic that one of the authors remembers from her elementary school days is learning to spell a new word, *geography,* by associating each letter of *geography* with the initial letter of each word in a sentence that her teacher presented: *George's eldest oldest girl rode a pig home yesterday.* Other examples similar to the previous example are (1) *Every good boy deserves favor* (representing the lines on the treble clef: EGBDF); (2) *Bless my dear Aunt Sally* (presenting the correct order for algebraic operations: brackets, multiply, divide, add, and subtract); and (3) *Do men ever visit Boston?* (relating the ranking of English titles: duke, marquis, earl, viscount, and baron). In some mnemonics, each letter of a word is important; for example, *HOMES* designates the first letter of each of the Great Lakes: Huron, Ontario, Michigan, Erie, and Superior, and *PAIL* lists the four types of skin cuts: puncture, abrasion, incision, and laceration.[33] To remember an extension number—for instance, 758—we might remember *SALT* with the *A* missing. Or, to remember a longer number (such as a social security number), we might break the number up into a series of two- or three-digit numbers. Still another device that we can use when we wish to remember the names of several people we have just met is to note—for each person—a distinctive facial feature and relate the feature to the person's name (through rhyming, defining, creating a ridiculous image, etc.). For instance, to remember the name Eileen Schroeder, concentrate on Eileen's eyes, and then picture one of her eyes leaning against Schroeder, one of Charles M. Schulz's cartoon characters. Lorayne, a memory training specialist, suggests an additional memory system, the link method. If we wanted to remember a shopping list, for example, we would link (or associate) the items by creating an absurd mental image. Suppose someone told us to purchase carrots, cigars, milk, and an all-purpose cleaner. Using the link method, we might mentally picture a carrot smoking a cigar and wiping up spilled milk with an all-purpose cleaner.[34] Mnemonic devices, limited only to our own creativity, can be useful memorizing strategies that can help us recall items in a sequence.

Following Oral Directions

A skill that is closely related to sequential ordering and that is considered necessary for comprehensive listeners to develop is the ability to follow oral directions. Lundsteen includes this skill in a list of comprehensive skills that are most frequently mentioned in listening literature.[35] Also, Brown and Carlsen include this skill as one of the five listening skills that their test measures.[36] Additionally, the Speech Communication Association has included this skill in its list of minimal competencies in speaking and listening for high school graduates.[37] Our need to develop this skill can readily be seen when we consider how frequently we are daily required to follow oral directions; we often need to apply this skill when we perform job tasks, order items introduced on the radio or television, perform household maintenance tasks, exercise, play a game unfamiliar to us, apply a medical treatment, and numerous other activities.

Not following oral directions in these as well as other areas can be costly—costly to us and to others. For example, a friend of ours, John, was recently told to buy ten fifty-cent combination lottery tickets for his boss. Rather than purchasing combination tickets, John bought straight tickets, one of which was 572, and the winning number that day was 752. This example is minor compared to other examples of errors caused by people not following oral directions. However, whether the listener be an airplane pilot, a medical surgeon, or our friend John, the problem is still the same: we often make costly errors because we do not listen carefully to oral directions.

To develop this skill, we must apply much of what we have learned to do when we develop the previously discussed skill—recalling items in a sequence; however, this new skill—one that, too, can be developed through our use of memory aids—often requires us to recall sentences and longer phrases rather than short phrases and words. We must carefully attend to the oral stimuli; by intensely concentrating, we can insure that the oral directions will be stored in our LTM. Also, practice—in improving our concentration ability as we listen to oral directions—can aid us in becoming more efficient in this skill.

Formulating Meaningful Questions

The final skill that we will discuss in this chapter is the skill of asking questions. On the surface, asking questions does not appear to be a listening skill; however, Lundsteen has found that *to formulate simple questions* is frequently included in listening scholars' lists of important comprehensive listening skills.[38] When we consider that the goal of comprehensive listening is to understand the sender's message, we realize that if we willingly ask a sender to clarify a point that we find confusing, we have a greater chance to reach our goal of understanding.

But, how often do we ask questions when we wish to have a point clarified or when we need additional information? Patterson and Cosgrove, investigating the frequency with which children ranging from preschoolers to fourth graders asked questions when they needed more information, found that only fourth graders spontaneously asked questions. These researchers have suggested that "although active, effective listening may often require students to ask questions, teachers may inadvertently foster the belief that good listening requires listeners to remain silent."[39] Patterson further stresses that not asking questions is not limited to elementary students; she has also found that few students ask questions in the courses she teaches at the University of Virginia. When she surveyed the students in her Introductory Child Psychology course, she found that although 94 percent of the students admitted to not having understood something presented in class at least once or twice, 70 percent said they had never asked a question in class. Among their reasons for not asking questions were "fear of looking stupid and a desire not to make themselves conspicuous."[40] Her students did not indicate that they did not ask questions because she did not create a climate conducive to questioning. We know, however, that the manner in which any sender (whether it be a teacher, parent, boss, etc.) responds to our questions can affect our willingness to ask that person questions. Nevertheless, if we have a sincere desire to become more effective comprehensive listeners, we must put aside our pride and discomfort and ask questions when we do not understand.

Once we have developed the willingness to ask questions, we also must learn when, how often, and how to ask questions. We should wait until the sender (whether it be a speaker, a boss, or a close friend) has completed his or her message before we ask questions; often, we interrupt (or wish to interrupt) someone so that we can ask a question at a time when, if we had just waited for the sender to finish, the sender would have answered our question in his or her message. The frequency with which we should ask questions lies somewhere between a car going 75 miles per hour and a car that is out of gas. Most of us know someone who interrupts to question much too often (and most likely perceives questioning as a substitute for listening rather than questioning as a follow-up to listening), and most of us know someone who questions so rarely that we wonder if he or she is even interested in what we are saying. Also, we should not ask questions that are irrelevant or distracting. Does it really matter whether we saw a furniture truck in front of our friend's house on Tuesday or Wednesday when our friend is describing his or her newly acquired chairs and couch? The manner in which we ask questions, too, is important. Hayakawa believes that good listeners ask questions that "avoid all implications (whether in tone of voice or wording) of skepticism or challenge or hostility. They must clearly be motivated by curiosity about the speaker's view."[41] Using a condescending or angry

When we ask a question, we must be
willing to listen to the answer.
Photo by Robert Tocha.

tone or asking a question that is loaded or is embarrassing to the speaker should
not be a part of effective listeners' communication behavior. Hayakawa further
suggests that the most useful kind of question for clarification may be one phrased
in this manner: " 'I am going to restate in my words what I think you mean.
Then would you mind telling me if I've understood you correctly?' "[42] Lastly,
when we do ask a question, we must be willing to listen to the answer—even if
we disagree with it or if the answer takes much longer than we had hoped it
would, for, after all, we ask questions so that we can increase our understanding
of the sender's message.

A Recommended Technique for Improving Understanding

We would like to conclude this chapter on comprehensive listening by describing
a technique that will help us check our understanding of a sender's message. The
need to test the quality of our understanding has been stressed by many people
who deal with helping others to communicate more effectively. Rogers, a well-
known psychotherapist, believes that the major barrier to interpersonal communication is our tendency to react to a highly emotional statement by evaluating
it from our own frame of reference. To avoid this barrier, he proposes that we

listen with understanding; that is, we try to see the expressed message from the sender's frame of reference.[43] Hayakawa stresses that understanding should also be our goal when we attend a conference; he points out that "too often, the fact that misunderstanding exists is not apparent until deeper misunderstandings have already occurred because of the original one."[44] Most of us have attended business conferences, civic meetings, or social events where we have listened to a heated discussion involving two people who were not discussing the same issue. The discussion starts with Mrs. Fleming making a statement that Mr. Burr hears differently than Mrs. Fleming intended. Mr. Burr tries to refute what he thought Mrs. Fleming said. Not understanding Mr. Burr's protest, Mrs. Fleming defends her original message with further statements. Mr. Burr then interprets these statements in the light of the original message that he misunderstood, and he responds by moving further away from Mrs. Fleming's original statement. The discussion becomes more and more heated, and the comprehensive listener's goal of understanding becomes more and more unreachable. Supporting Rogers's view, Hayakawa suggests that we can avoid such entanglements if we engage in "entering actively and imaginatively into the other fellow's situation and trying to understand a frame of reference different from your own."[45] Two others who recognize the importance of checking our understanding are Edelson and Venema, who help married couples ease problems of marital strife. Edelson, a University of Wisconsin social scientist, believes that accuracy is the one communication ingredient that is really important. When recommending basic steps toward improved communication, he suggests, "Make sure everything you said was accurate and it was understood . . . it's okay to ask questions if they [sic] understood what you were saying."[46] He further stresses that being accurate is the responsibility of both the speaker and the listener, who has to ask, "Am I hearing that right?"[47] Venema, a clinical psychologist, recommends the following approach for developing better understanding:

> An active, involved listener does a lot of talking. He uses words to "mirror back" what he thinks the other is communicating. This approach permits correction of errors. It also sends a message back to the speaker: "This person is really trying to hear what I'm saying."[48]

Each of these people we have just cited recognizes the need for improved understanding, and each has suggested some guidelines we can use to test the quality of our understanding; however, Rogers's technique is probably the one that is most frequently recommended by communication scholars.

Rogers's technique is one that we highly recommend. There is one rule that must be instituted when we are practicing this technique: " 'Each person can speak up for himself only *after* he has first restated the ideas and feelings of the previous speaker accurately and to that speaker's satisfaction.' "[49] Simply stated, the technique involves two people engaging in a dialogue; as the two people discuss some item of interest, the listener must restate what he or she thinks the speaker has said to the speaker's satisfaction before the listener (who then becomes the speaker) can contribute a further idea to the discussion. This will be a slow process, but we will find this is an excellent technique for improving our understanding—which is the goal of the comprehensive listener.

Summary

In this chapter, we have examined comprehensive listening—listening for understanding. We have illustrated that comprehensive listening plays a significant role in all phases of our lives and that many variables—including memory, concentration, size of vocabulary, age, intelligence, motivation, scholastic achievement, speaking ability, reading comprehension, verbal ability, language and study skills, rate of presentation, and cultural status—appear to be slightly to moderately related to listening comprehension; however, we have stressed that additional research investigating these variables, as well as others, must be conducted for us to determine the specific variables that are most directly related to listening comprehension. Additionally, we have listed, discussed, and suggested ways to improve eight skills that appear to be involved in comprehensive listening: capitalizing on the differential between speech speed and thought speed, listening for main ideas, listening for significant details, drawing justifiable inferences, being an effective notetaker, recalling items in a sequence, following oral directions, and formulating meaningful questions. Lastly, we have described a technique that will help us to improve our understanding and, thus, help us reach our goal as comprehensive listeners.

Activities to Try

1. Deliberately try to improve your concentration ability in the classes that are giving you the most difficulty. Keep a log of your concentration habits. List the times you started listening and the times you found yourself "tuning out." Also, list why you stopped listening and what you found yourself thinking about when you realized you were not concentrating on the class discussion or lecture. Keep this log for a designated period of time and then turn it in to the instructor.[50]
2. Prepare a statement that includes at least one word with which many college students would be unfamiliar. Read your statement to the class (only once), and the listeners are to identify the unfamiliar word(s) and guess at its/their meaning(s). When a student guesses correctly, that student is to explain what contextual clues led him or her to make the proper guess. When a student guesses incorrectly, another student should be given the opportunity to define the missed word. Students are then to discuss how size of vocabulary affects listening comprehension.[51]

3. Five or six class members (assuming fictitious names and backgrounds) will form a receiving line. Other class members (designated as guests) will go through the receiving line. Each member of the receiving line will introduce each guest to the person standing by him or her by stating the name of the guest and the name of and some background information on the person next in line. Each guest will state that person's name and comment on the given background information.

4. Class members will roleplay a situation involving three participants. One will be assigned the role of foremen or boss, and two will be assigned the role of new employeees. The foreman will teach a set of new procedures to the first new employee. That employee will then teach the procedures to the second new employee. The rest of the students will note the problems involved in the following (and perhaps the giving) of oral directions.

5. Several class members will be designated as senders. They will prepare specific, step-by-step directions for completing some simple task such as putting staples in a stapler, opening a window, opening a bottle. Each sender will be paired with a receiver. One at a time, each listener will follow—in front of the class—the sender's directions. The sender can not add directions that he or she does not have written down, and the receiver cannot do anything that she or he has not been told to do; the receiver cannot communicate with the sender, either. Participants will then discuss how this exercise has helped them to discover the difficulty of accurately giving and following oral directions.[52]

Notes

1. Robert L. Montgomery, "How to Improve Your Memory," *U.S. News and World Report* 87 (August 27, 1979): 55.
2. K. Anders Ericsson, William G. Chase, and Steve Faloon, "Acquisition of a Memory Skill," *Science* 208 (June 6, 1980): 1182.
3. Charles Robert Petrie, Jr., "The Listener," in *Listening: Readings,* ed. Sam Duker (New York: Scarecrow Press, 1966), p. 337.
4. Evan L. Wright, "The Construction of a Test of Listening Comprehension for the Second, Third, and Fourth Grades" (Ph.D. diss., Washington University, 1957), *Dissertation Abstracts* 17 (1957): 2226–2227; Richard Hampleman, "Comparison of Listening and Reading Comprehension Ability of Fourth and Sixth Grade Pupils," *Elementary English* 35 (January 1958): 49–53; Vern L. Farrow, "An Experimental Study of Listening Attention at the Fourth, Fifth, and Sixth Grade" (Ph.D. diss., University of Oregon, 1963), *Dissertation Abstracts* 24 (1964): 3146; James I. Brown and G. Robert Carlsen, *Brown-Carlsen Listening Comprehension Test* (New York: Harcourt, Brace and World, 1955), p. 15; John Caffrey, "Auding Ability at the Secondary Level," *Education* 75 (January 1955): 308; Edwyna F. Condon, "An Analysis of the Difference between Good and Poor Listeners in Grades Nine, Eleven, and Thirteen" (Ph.D. diss., University of Kansas, 1965), *Dissertation Abstracts* 26 (1965): 3106; Allen G. Erickson, "Can Listening Efficiency Be Improved?" *Journal of Communication* 4 (Winter 1954): 128–132; Althea Beery et al., *Sequential Tests*

of *Educational Progress: Listening Comprehension* (Princeton, New Jersey: Educational Testing Service, 1957).

5. A correlation coefficient is a commonly used numerical measure of the degree of relationship between two or more variables. The correlation coefficient ranges in value from -1.00 for perfect negative correlation through .00 for no correlation to $+1.00$ for complete positive correlation; thus, a low correlation coefficient indicates a weak relationship between variables, and a high correlation coefficient indicates a strong relationship between variables.

6. Erickson, "Can Listening Efficiency Be Improved?" p. 131.

7. Charles M. Kelly, "Listening: Complexity of Activities—and a Unitary Skill?" *Speech Monographs* 34 (November 1967): 456; Henry T. Moore, "The Attention Value of Lecturing without Notes," *Journal of Educational Psychology* 10 (1919): 467–469; Franklin H. Knower, David Phillips, and Fern Keoppel, "Studies in Listening to Informative Speaking," *Journal of Abnormal and Social Psychology* 40 (January 1945): 82–88; Daniel W. Mullin, "An Experimental Study of Retention in Educational Television," *Speech Monographs* 24 (March 1957): 31–38; Ralph G. Nichols, "Factors in Listening Comprehension," *Speech Monographs* 15 (1948): 161; David G. Ryans, "Motivation in Learning," in *Growth, Teaching, and Learning*, ed. H. H. Remers et al. (New York: Harper and Brothers, 1957), p. 125; Charles T. Brown, "Studies in Listening Comprehension," *Speech Monographs* 26 (November 1959): 288–294.

8. John A. Haberland, "A Comparison of Listening Tests with Standardized Tests," *Journal of Educational Research* 52 (April 1959): 301; Robert J. Baldauf, "A Study of a Measure of Listening Comprehension and Its Relation to the School Achievement of Fifth Grade Pupils" (Ph.D. Diss., University of Colorado, 1960), *Dissertation Abstracts* 21 (1960): 2979.

9. Joel Stark, "An Investigation of the Relationship of the Vocal and Communicative Aspects of Speech Competency with Listening Comprehension" (Ph.D. diss., New York University, 1956), *Dissertation Abstracts* 17 (1957): 696; Annette Vister Evans, "Listening Related to Speaking in the First Grade" (M. A. thesis, Atlanta University, 1960).

10. Erickson, "Can Listening Efficiency Be Improved?", p. 131; Sam Duker, "Listening and Reading," *Elementary School Journal* 65 (March 1965): 322.

11. Edward J. J. Kramer, "The Relationships of the Wechsler-Bellevue and A.C.E. Intelligence Tests with Performance Scores in Speaking and the Brown-Carlsen Listening Comprehension Test" (Ph.D. diss., Florida State University, 1955), *Dissertation Abstracts* 15 (1955): 2599; Ramon Ross, "A Look at Listeners," *Elementary School Journal* 64 (April 1964): 370.

12. Brown and Carlsen, *Brown-Carlsen Listening Comprehension Test*, p. 18.

13. Charles Robert Petrie, Jr., "Listening and Organization," *Central States Speech Journal* 15 (February 1964): 8–9.

14. Thomas Wood Smith, "Cultural Bias and Listening," in *Listening: Readings*, ed. Sam Duker, p. 128; Ramon Ross, "A Look at Listeners," p. 370.

15. Ralph G. Nichols, "Listening Is a 10-Part Skill," *Nation's Business* 45 (July 1957): 4.

16. Paul W. Keller, "Major Findings in Listening in the Past Ten Years," *Journal of Communication* 10 (March 1960): 34.

17. Sanford E. Gerber, "Dichotic and Diotic Presentations of Speeded Speech," *Journal of Communication* 18 (September 1968): 272–282.

18. Grant Fairbanks, Newman Guttman, and Murray S. Miron, "Auditory Comprehension of Repeated High-Speed Messages," *Journal of Speech and Hearing Disorders* 22 (March 1957): 20–22.

19. David B. Orr, "Time Compressed Speech—A Perspective," *Journal of Communication* 18 (September 1968): 288–292.

20. Emerson Foulke et al., "The Compression of Rapid Speech by the Blind," *Exceptional Children* 29 (November 1962): 134–141.

21. Emerson Foulke, ed., *Proceedings: Third Louisville Conference on Rate Controlled Speech* (New York: American Foundation for the Blind, 1975).

22. Linda Olsen, "Technology Humanized: The Rate-Controlled Tape Recorder," *Media and Methods* 15 (January 1979): 67.

23. For more specific information regarding the use of compressed speech in business, education, and public services, contact Variable Speech Control (VSC) Corporation, 185 Berry Street, San Francisco, California 94107; the telephone number is 415/495–6100—TELEX 340–328.

24. James MacLachlan, "What People Really Think of Fast Talkers," *Psychology Today* 13 (November 1979): 113–117.

25. The address and phone number of Variable Speech Control Corporation (VSC) can be found in footnote number 23 of this chapter.

26. The address of AmBiChron is 67 Smith Street, Lynbrook, New York 11563; the telephone number is 516/599–3489.

27. The address of Lexicon is 60 Turner Street, Waltham, Massachusetts 02154; the telephone number is 617/891–6790.

28. To receive information regarding the ordering of rate-controlled recorded speech and/or descriptions of commercially available speech compressors, contact Emerson Foulke, Perceptual Alternative Laboratory, University of Louisville—Graduate School, Louisville, Kentucky 40292, or call 502/588–6722.

29. Roy M. Berko, Andrew D. Wolvin, and Darlyn R. Wolvin, *Communicating: A Social and Career Focus* (Boston: Houghton Mifflin Company, 1977), pp. 234–241.

30. Carl H. Weaver, *Human Listening: Processes and Behavior* (Indianapolis: Bobbs-Merrill Company, 1972), p. 70.

31. Ralph G. Nichols, "Do We Know How to Listen? Practical Helps in a Modern Age," *Speech Teacher* 10 (March 1961): 122.

32. Brown and Carlsen, *Brown-Carlsen Listening Comprehension Test,* p. 4.

33. Scot Morris, "Games," *Omni* 11 (March 1980): 144–145, 126; Michael Olmert, "It's Hard Enough to Say It, Let Alone Remember It," *Smithsonian* 8 (October 1977): 172.

34. V. J. Rex, "Memory Massage," *Future,* September/October 1980, p. 34.

35. Sara W. Lundsteen, *Listening: Its Impact on Reading and the Other Language Arts* (Illinois: NCTE/ERIC, 1971), pp. 52–53.

36. Brown and Carlsen, *Brown-Carlsen Listening Comprehension Test,* p. 4.

37. Ronald E. Bassett, Nilwon Whittington, and Ann Stanton-Spicer, "The Basics in Speaking and Listening for High School Graduates: What Should Be Assessed?" *Communication Education* 27 (November 1978): 298.

38. Lundsteen, *Listening: Its Impact on Reading and the Other Language Arts,* pp. 52–53.

39. Charlotte J. Patterson, "Teaching Children to Listen," *Today's Education* 67 (April/Mary 1978): 53.

40. *Ibid.*
41. S. I. Hayakawa, "How to Attend a Conference," *ETC* 3 (Autumn 1955): 5–9.
42. *Ibid.*
43. Carl R. Rogers and F. J. Roethlisberger, "Barriers and Gateways to Communication," *Harvard Business Review* 30 (July 1952): 46–52.
44. S. I. Hayakawa, "How to Attend a Conference."
45. *Ibid.*
46. "To Ease Marital Strife, Try Really Listening," *The Evening Sun* 15 November 1976, p. A-3.
47. *Ibid.*
48. Marion Wells, "Listening Says You Really Care," *Grit* 15 January 1978, p. 16.
49. Rogers and Roethlisberger, "Barriers and Gateways to Communication," p. 48.
50. Andrew D. Wolvin and Carolyn Gwynn Coakley, *Listening Instruction* (Urbana, Illinois: ERIC Clearinghouse on Reading and Communication Skills, 1979), p. 16.
51. *Ibid.,* pp. 16–17.
52. *Ibid.,* pp. 25–26.

concepts you will encounter

Therapeutic Listening
Empathy
Sounding Board
Defensive Climate
Supportive Climate
Trust
Active Listening
Risk
Nondirective Listening
Paraphrasing
Feelings

skills you should develop

Avoiding Evaluative Feedback
Becoming an Active Listener
Listening with Empathy
Listening Nondirectively
Developing a Supportive
   Communication Climate
Paraphrasing Messages
Listening for Feelings

therapeutic listening

7

The fourth purpose of listening, therapeutic listening, requires the listener to discriminate and to comprehend the sender's message while providing the sender with a "sounding board" to talk through his or her problem. The therapeutic listener provides this sounding board without guiding or directing the sender in his or her solutions in any way.

Suppose, for instance, that your friend Ron is having difficulty adjusting to a new supervisor at work. Ron has become discouraged with repeated attempts to develop a good working relationship with this supervisor. It is as if the two have a "personality conflict." So Ron comes to you for help.

A natural tendency may be for you to tell your friend how *you* would deal with the situation—to give him directions for resolving or avoiding the conflict. You might suggest, for instance, that he should ask for a transfer to another office. But does this kind of advice really help a friend? Unless you know the supervisor and have been in the office, are you really in a position to give direct advice to your friend?

The situation, then, may well call for a therapeutic listener. As a friend, you can listen with empathy (by putting yourself in Ron's place) as he explains his problem. While serving as a "sounding board" for your friend, you can keep him talking through your verbal and nonverbal responses which communicate to him that you are listening, that you care, and that you understand. It is important to note at the outset, however, that we are not advocating that listeners play "amateur psychiatrists." Problems of a serious psychological nature require more than an empathetic friend. Persons with serious problems should be referred to professional therapists.

The Need for Therapeutic Listening

The need for an empathetic listener probably resides in most of us. It certainly is a characteristic of alienated urban America. In San Francisco, a firm entitled "Conversation" has been established to fill this need for therapeutic listeners. For five dollars a half hour, the firm provides listeners who let people talk to them. The proliferation of telephone "hot lines" and "listening posts" is yet another manifestation of this great need for therapeutic listeners.

The need for effective therapeutic listening has been recognized by many experts. Dr. Robert Wicks, a psychologist-author, suggests that he "would like to see people not quickly sending everyone to a professional."[1] Instead, Wicks urges people to resist the impulse to give advice and instead spend time listening to the person's problem.

Beier and Valens, in their interesting work on *People Reading,* stress the importance of listening to your children:

> Listening to a young person can easily be an act of love. Listening with concern but without judging is an art, and it helps the child explore his motivations, his style, and the compromises he has so far achieved. . . . . It means giving him a safe place where he can speak at his own speed and explore new options, however unrealistic they may appear to us.[2]

Psychologists recognize that the importance of listening to children extends to the teenage, adolescent years. Psychologist-author, Manford Sonstegard, has developed a series of workshops on "Listening to Teens." In his work, Sonstegard advises parents to be willing to listen to their teens "without always making value judgments. And be willing to concede that parents don't always know the right answer."[3]

While workshops on family communication, which stresses listening, are popular, so, too, are workshops on couple communication. In one such workshop, Dr. Jeffrey Moss, a social worker, conducts a seminar on "Communication Skill Building and Problem Solving in the Couple Relationship." Moss contends that listening with empathy is important because being a couple "is never easy." Feelings become hurt, angers mount, disagreements grow, and as a result there is a need to give vent to these feelings."[4] Moss stresses that effective listening does not require that you take on your partner's problems. "Rather, to be a good listener is to be a sounding board for your mate's thoughts and feelings. You help the other person clarify feelings which have plagued him/her."[5]

The need for listening with empathy extends to the workplace. B. O. Sorrell notes that the effective manager must "convey the idea that he understands and appreciates what the speaker said. This requires listening with empathy."[6] Teachers also are encouraged to listen with empathy in order to help their students grow as persons. To develop an atmosphere in which student self-exploration is possible, teachers should demonstrate "understanding of and skill at communicating these concepts of empathy, respect, and genuineness."[7]

While it is evident that therapeutic listening serves a major role in interpersonal relationships in American society, it may not be so evident that we *are* able to function as therapeutic listeners when friends and family members come to us with problems (provided that these problems are not of a serious psychological nature). A recent study by two psychologists compared the results of two groups of patients who suffered neurotic depression or anxiety reactions. One group was treated by psychotherapists, and the other group was treated by college professors who demonstrated ability to form understanding relationships. The results of the study indicated that the patients treated by professors showed, on the average, as much improvement as patients treated by professional therapists.[8] It is possible for people to serve a therapeutic function as listeners.

Skills Involved in Therapeutic Listening

Avoiding Evaluative Feedback

The greatest barrier to effective therapeutic listening is what Carl Rogers has identified (as was discussed in chapter 6) as the greatest of all listening barriers—the human tendency to evaluate. Rogers elaborates on this barrier:

> The major barrier to mutual interpersonal communication is our very natural tendency to judge, to evaluate, to approve (or disapprove) the statement of the other person or the other group. . . . Suppose someone, commenting on this discussion, makes the statement, "I didn't like what that man said." What will you respond? Almost invariably your reply will be either approval or disapproval of the attitude expressed. Either you respond, "I didn't either; I thought it was terrible," or else you need to reply, "Oh, I thought it was really good." In other words, your primary reaction is to evaluate it from *your* point of view, your own frame of reference.[9]

This tendency to evaluate is an obstacle for therapeutic listeners to overcome so that they do not provide any sort of evaluative feedback—positive or negative—which might influence speakers toward a particular direction. The role of the listener at this level is strictly to serve as a sounding board, so the speaker must direct his or her own solution to the problem.

Becoming An Active Listener

Rogers (with Richard Farson) suggests that the therapeutic listener should work to become an "active listener." The listener should actively attempt to "grasp the facts and the feelings in what he hears" and try, by this active listening, to "help the speaker work out his own problems."[10] To develop this skill, Rogers and Farson emphasize that there are problems to overcome. This type of listening carries with it considerable personal risk. To listen with empathy to another's point of view—to truly recognize and understand the other person—may lead to the listener's making personal changes. Giving up, even for a short time, one's point of view for another's point of view may indeed be risky.[11]

This risk extends to hearing what we do not want to hear, perhaps extending to personal attacks on ourselves as listeners and, certainly, to the discussion of information which personally may be offensive. Thus, it is important to set aside these personal responses in order to truly empathize with the other person's problem.

Rogers and Farson suggest that it may be difficult to listen not only to these negative expressions but also to positive feelings. Emotional outbursts of praise and joy can be difficult for some persons to handle. Much of this problem, particularly in management, may stem from our social conditioning. As listeners, we may well hear negative complaints and criticism much more frequently than positive reinforcement. Indeed, persons of authority—managers, teachers—probably do not pay enough attention to communicating praise and reinforcement. Instead, many of us hear only negative messages from superiors.

Listening with Empathy

Because of these critical, complaining messages, we may have difficulty functioning as therapeutic listeners who listen with empathy. In an early work on empathetic listening, Charles Kelly pointed out that empathetic listening is primarily a matter of listening objectively. Both the deliberative (critical) and empathetic listener "has the desire to understand the speaker first, and, as a result, tries to take the appropriate action" while the deliberative listener first has the desire to critically evaluate the message[12] It is necessary, then, to put aside all critical standards and judgments in order to perform as a true empathetic, therapeutic listener. Further, it is important to be nondirective while serving in this capacity.

Listening Nondirectively

In order to be effectively nondirective, we should follow some suggestions which Ralph Nichols formulated for effective nondirective listening.[13] Nichols's first point must be the beginning: have faith in the ability of speakers to solve their own problems. This basic assumption underlies the entire premise of therapeutic listening. Essentially, it is a valid assumption. Most problems can be solved if we have the opportunity to talk them through. Should the problem be great enough to require clinical, professional assistance, of course, the therapeutic listener should not undertake to deal with it. A problem which requires psychological attention should be referred to the properly-trained therapist.

Suppose David, a friend of yours, has a problem with a particular class in school and is in need of a therapeutic listener. In this role, you might be able to see that your friend can handle the problem if he can just talk it through. So, instead of telling David what you would do to tackle the problem, you listen with empathy while he draws his own conclusions as to how to deal with the problem. Perhaps, through self-disclosure of the problem, he sees that he needs to spend more time studying. Or perhaps he needs to use his study time more productively, really concentrating on the homework. Maybe he even needs to sharpen his listening skills to better follow the material in the professor's lectures. Whatever the solution, it is clear that David can handle his own study problem without your direction. But without your empathetic listening, he would not have had the opportunity to articulate the problem and realize how to deal with it.

A second point emphasized by Nichols is that the effective therapeutic listener should take time to listen. The task of talking through a problem cannot be hurried; it will take time for speakers to arrive at their own solutions. They may never arrive at solutions if they do not have ample time to analyze their problems. If you assume the role of therapeutic listener, you must allow yourself the time to sit down with the speaker and really concentrate on that person's message. If you do not have the time at the particular point that therapeutic listening is required, it would be wise to explain your lack of time to the speaker and not enter into a rushed session—such an approach would be neither productive for the speaker nor satisfying for the listener.

One of our students became especially skilled at listening with empathy. She was able to send appropriate responses to truly serve as a "sounding board" for all her friends on campus. She became so noted for her therapeutic listening skill, however, that she had to spend practically all of her time in her dorm room listening to friends. Eventually, this time became counterproductive for her, as she was unable to find time for herself and her studies. Consequently, she came to realize that there are situations when it is just not possible to take the time to be a truly effective "sounding board" for others.

As a third suggestion for nondirective listening, Nichols recommends that the listener be attentive. Actually, effective therapeutic listening can go beyond just attending to listening with empathy—putting yourself in the speaker's place. A good therapeutic listener will try to understand the orientation—the point of view of the speaker—in order to better comprehend what the speaker is describing.

Mike, for instance, comes to you with a problem he is having with Ella, his girlfriend. She is working hard in school to get the necessary grades and academic record to qualify for medical school. Mike, too, wants to go to medical school, but he has a natural aptitude for his academic pursuits, so he does not have to spend the time Ella does on school work. In order to deal with Mike's problem, you will have to listen with empathy, to understand that Mike does not have to spend as much time as most people do but that his academic career is still important to him. As you listen to Mike, then, you will want to try to put yourself in his place and recognize his frustrations with Ella's more typical study habits.

The skilled therapeutic listener can create a warm bond of empathy with the speaker through nonverbal cues of concern, interest, and attentiveness. Nichols cautions, however, that verbal reactions in a nondirective setting should be of only three forms: (1) eloquent and encouraging grunts such as "huh" or "uh huh"; (2) silence, nodding the head; and (3) restatements of what has been said in the form of a question.

This third response should be handled with care, but it can be quite effective. Suppose Dianne has just said, "I don't think I can get through the test tomorrow. I'm not prepared." Your response, as a therapeutic listener, should not be, "Why aren't you prepared?" Instead, to let Dianne find her own solution, you might respond with the question, "You don't feel prepared?" Such a response can serve to get the speaker to open up and elaborate on her feelings without specifically channeling her thoughts to one particular point.

Developing a Supportive Communication Climate
Instead of responding as Nichols suggests, however, most of us offer responses which can have the effect of closing off a speaker's disclosure of a problem. Dr. Thomas Gordon, for example, in his popular *Parent Effectiveness Training,* has categorized the way people typically respond to children's messages. We may respond in these ways:
1. Ordering, directing, commanding
2. Warning, admonishing, threatening

3. Exhorting, moralizing, preaching
4. Advising, giving solutions or suggestions
5. Lecturing, teaching, giving logical arguments
6. Judging, criticizing, disagreeing, blaming
7. Praising, agreeing
8. Name calling, ridiculing, shaming
9. Interpreting, analyzing, diagnosing
10. Reassuring, sympathizing, consoling, supporting
11. Probing, questioning, interrogating
12. Withdrawing, distracting, humoring, diverting

Gordon notes that these "typical twelve" responses are highly inappropriate as therapeutic responses, the very kinds of responses that professional therapists and counselors work to avoid.[14]

Teachers, as well as parents, should be aware of the messages they send and make an effort to create an open, supportive communication climate. Theodore Wright notes that the listener may become defensive if the communicator, through verbal and nonverbal messages, seems to be evaluating or judging the listener. On the other hand, if the listener "thinks that the speaker regards him as an equal and is being open and spontaneous, for example, the evaluativeness in a message will be neutralized and perhaps not even perceived."[15]

To understand how to avoid a defensive communication climate, the listener should note the classic study of communication climate conducted by Jack R. Gibb. Gibb identified six types of characteristics which can arouse defensiveness and six contrasting characteristics which can produce/create supportive communication climates:

Defensive Climates	*Supportive Climates*
1. Evaluation	1. Description
2. Control	2. Problem Orientation
3. Strategy	3. Spontaneity
4. Neutrality	4. Empathy
5. Superiority	5. Equality
6. Certainty	6. Provisionalism[16]

Essentially, Gibb's categories support the point that a directive, authoritarian approach to responding will, indeed, create a defensive communication climate. The therapeutic listener, then, who wants to create an open, empathetic communication climate will attempt to respond supportively.

It is possible to contrast the characteristics with examples of responses:
1. Evaluation: "I don't think you have a clear idea of what you want to do."
   Descriptive: "You are concerned that you're not sure what step to take?"
2. Control: "Let's handle it this way."
   Problem Orientation: "How would you prefer to proceed?"
3. Strategy: "I'm sure you don't feel that's necessary."
   Spontaneity: "You have an idea there!"

4. Neutrality: "I don't care. What do you want?"
   Empathy: "I'll bet you have some ideas for handling it."
5. Superiority: "Well, I would do this."
   Equality: "Let's see what we can do."
6. Certainty: "Of course, it's the only way."
   Provisionalism: "One approach could incorporate that procedure."

As therapeutic listeners, then, we should be aware of the responses we send and work to develop an open, supportive communication climate in which the sender will feel comfortable expressing the problems and concerns he or she may have.

The development of an open, supportive communication climate is facilitated by trust in the relationship. As the sender in the communication discloses his or her feelings and concerns, that person becomes vulnerable, risking evaluation, ridicule, or rejection from you. It is important, therefore, to work to help the person feel "safe" in communicating the problem and to recognize that there is an element of risk in revealing so much to you. The key to establishing a trusting relationship with this person is to be trustworthy—communicating to the sender that you will not take advantage of his or her vulnerability in self-disclosing to you. David Johnson describes communicating this trust:

> . . . the expression of warmth towards the other person in a relationship builds a high level of interpersonal trust because it increases the other person's expectations that you will respond with acceptance and support when he self-discloses. In addition, the congruence of your verbal statements, nonverbal cues such as facial expression and tone of voice, and your behavior will affect the other person's perception of your trustworthiness.[17]

Paraphrasing Messages

An effective way to develop skill in listening with empathy is to strive to provide speakers with feedback consisting, in essence, of paraphrases of their messages. As we noted in chapter 6, training in paraphrasing is useful because total involvement in the speaker's message is crucial to the satisfactory reiteration of the speaker's statement. Brammer suggests that skill in paraphrasing develops if you work to (1) listen to the message; (2) restate the message in a simple, concise summary; and (3) ask for a cue or response from the other person as to the accuracy or helpfulness of the paraphrase.[18] A person, for instance, may tell you: "I really can't get along with Jerry, my co-worker. He's always trying to find things wrong with my work so that he'll look better in the eyes of the boss." You could paraphrase this message by saying, "You feel that Jerry criticizes your work so that his work will look better?" Such a response can enable you to communicate that you are listening carefully, and it can enable you to clarify or check any messages that may not be very specific.

For a person to function as an effective therapeutic listener, Nichols recommends that he or she never probe for additional facts. Such a suggestion is consistent with the nondirective focus of therapeutic listening, but you may find times when it is necessary to use nondirective responses to probe to get the

Paraphrasing speakers' messages
enables us to communicate that we
are listening attentively and nondirectively.
Photo by Robert Tocha.

speaker to go beyond superficial statements. Your friend with the examination problem, for instance, may need to look more broadly at her study habits in order to revise her methods of test preparation. Only through careful indirect probing can you get the speaker to come to a realization of the actual problem.

Listening for Feelings

An important step in the exploration of the speaker's problem is to uncover the feelings involved. Listening to the expression of feelings is difficult because it takes so much time and because our language is not very helpful with expressions of feelings. We do not have enough words to express our feelings. One can see the inadequacy of our feeling vocabulary just by reviewing a list of words we use to describe unpleasant and pleasant feeling states:[19]

Unpleasant Feeling States

Feelings of Anger

aggravated	hostile
angry	intolerant
annoyed	irritated
belligerent	mad

bitter
bugged
cool
cruel
ennerved
enraged
furious
hateful

mean
peeved
perturbed
resentful
spiteful
vengeful
vindictive

Feelings of Sadness

abandoned
alienated
alone
ashamed
awful
blue
crushed
defeated
depressed
despondent
disappointed
down
forelorn
foresaken

grief
hopeless
humiliated
hurt
lonely
low
neglected
rejected
sad
small
sorrow
unhappy
unloved (able)
worthless

Feelings of Fear

afraid
alarmed
anxious
apprehensive
desperation
embarrassed
fearful
frightened
horrified
insecure

intimidated
nervous
overwhelmed
panicky
restless
scared
shy
tense
threatened
timid
uneasy
worried

Feelings of Inadequacy

broken
cowardly
crippled

incompetent
ineffective
inferior

deficient
demoralized
disabled
feeble
helpless
impotent
inadequate

paralyzed
powerless
small
useless
vulnerable
weak

Feelings of Stress

ambivalent
anxious
baffled
bewildered
bothered
caught
confused
conflicted
disgusted
dissatisfied
distressed
disturbed
doubtful
exposed

frustrated
futile
helpless
hopeless
nervous
overwhelmed
perplexed
puzzled
skeptical
trapped
uncomfortable
unsure
upset
vulnerable

Pleasant Feeling States

Feelings of Happiness

aglow
calm
content
elated
enthused
excited
fantastic
gay
glad
good

great
happy
joyous
overjoyed
pleased
proud
satisfied
thrilled
wonderful

Feelings of Love, Caring

affable
affectionate
altruistic

genuine
giving
humane

amiable
caring
close
concerned
considerate
cooperative
devoted
empathic
forgiving
friendly
fulfilled

intimate
kind
love (able)
peaceful
sensitive
sympathy
tender
warm(th)
whole

Feelings of Adequacy

able
adequate
bold
brave
capable
competent
confident
effective
fearless

healthy
important
nervy
peerless
powerful
robust
secure
self-assured
stable
strong

Even though most of us have an inadequate feeling vocabularly, the effective therapeutic listener can help the sender express feelings as meaningfully as possible. It is important to keep in mind Nichols's advice, as it reinforces Carl Rogers's point—never evaluate what has been said. If you believe the speaker can talk through a problem to his or her own solution, then you must let that person seek his or her own advice—not provide a "crutch" by offering judgments so that the friend does not have to come up with personal solutions.

Earl Koile recommends that we check out our own reactions if we are attempting to listen without criticizing or judging. As we are attempting to listen for understanding in a conversation or a discussion, he suggests that we see if we can say, "Yes, I understand or I am trying to understand your ideas or how you feel."[20] Koile notes that if we have the intent to listen with understanding, we are likely to convey that attitude to others in the communication.

The ability to solve our own problems makes for individual strength and satisfaction, the real advantage of therapeutic listening. While what we have described sounds clinical, and indeed the term "therapeutic" is clinical, we are really urging empathetic, helpful listening practices. A desire to serve in such a capacity and the ability to be a true "sounding board" for the speaker can enable an individual listener to function effectively as a therapeutic listener.

We listen with our hearts.
When I listen with the heart
I stop playing the game of non-listening.
In other words,
I step inside the other's skin;
I walk in his shoes;
I attempt to see things from his point-of-view;
I establish eye contact;
I give him conscious attention;
I reflect my understanding of his words;
I question;
I attempt to clarify.
Gently,
I draw the other out
as his lips stumble over words,
as his face becomes flushed,
as he turns his face aside.
I make the other feel that
I understand that he is important,
that I am grateful that he trusts me enough
to share deep, personal feelings with me.
I grant him worth.[21]

Summary

In this chapter, we have described some techniques for therapeutic listening—listening to provide a "sounding board" to allow a person to talk through a problem to his or her own solution. Effective therapeutic listening requires listening with comprehension and with empathy (putting yourself into the other person's perspective) in order to be the sounding board. A good therapeutic listener is nondirective, providing only the kind of responses which will keep the person talking without charting the course of his or her comments.

While we recognize the tremendous need for therapeutic listeners today, particularly as people need "someone to talk to," we have stressed the difficulty of this type of listening. The successful therapeutic listener must have both the time and the patience to assume the role of sounding board and the faith that the person is, indeed, able to come to grips with this problem and derive his or her own solution to it. Consequently, it is important not to play "amateur psychiatrist." The therapeutic listener should deal only with those problems which do not have serious psychological consequences. The rewards for listening with empathy, however, can be great, especially as you contribute to the growth of another human being.

Activities to Try

1. If you have a "Hot Line" telephone counseling referral service in your community, arrange to attend one of the training sessions where volunteers are taken through the principles of listening with empathy. What principles are stressed? What are the differences in listening with empathy over the telephone and listening with empathy to a person face-to-face?
2. Allow yourself to practice techniques of therapeutic listening. Permit a friend to talk with you about a problem (nothing of a serious psychological nature) related to his or her family, his or her school work, a friend, etc. Listen to the problem therapeutically, providing a "sounding board" for your friend's problem. Employ only nondirective responses such as those recommended by Nichols. Provide time for your friend to come up with his or her own solution. After the listening experience, ask your friend how he or she felt about your role as a therapeutic listener. Have him or her react before you disclose the techniques you attempted to utilize. How do *you* feel about the experience? Were you an effective therapeutic listener? Why or why not? What will you do differently the next time you attempt to function as a therapeutic listener?
3. Arrange to interview a professional counselor. Ask him or her about his or her therapeutic listening techniques. Does he or she use nondirective responses? How does he or she listen with empathy and yet maintain a professional "doctor-patient" detachment? Does he or she find that the development of therapeutic listening skills improves over time?
4. Practice listening with understanding in order to develop skill in empathetic listening. As someone talks with you about a problem, paraphrase the person's messages. Using effective reflective responses, restate what he or she has said. Reiterate his or her "feeling" messages as well.
5. Turn to the list of feeling words in the chapter. Expand the list with as many words as you can add. Why is it so difficult to handle such words? Are you able to come up with as many positive as negative words? Why?
6. Roleplay communication problems that you have personally encountered recently. During the roleplaying, practice therapeutic listening. Following the roleplaying, discuss the important aspects and skills surrounding therapeutic listening.

Notes

1. Robert Wicks, television interview with The Christophers, New York City, quoted in "Listening: First Aid for the Troubled Mind," *Grit,* 25 May 1980, p. 27.
2. Ernest G. Beier and Evans G. Valens, *People Reading* (New York: Stein and Day, 1975), p. 154.
3. Carol Krucoff, "Families: Listening to Teens," *The Washington Post* 17 June 1980, p. B-5.
4. Josephine Novak, "In Touch," *The Evening Sun* 6 October 1980, p. C-2.

5. *Ibid.*
6. B. D. Sorrell, "Is Anybody Listening?" *Data Management* 13 (December 1975): 34.
7. Lynette Long, *Listening/Responding* (Monterey, California: Brooks/Cole Publishing Company, 1978), p. 2.
8. Hans D. Strupp and Suzanne W. Hadley, "Specific vs. Nonspecific Factors in Psychotherapy," *Archives of General Psychiatry* 36 (September 1979); 1125.
9. Carl R. Rogers and F. J. Roethlisberger, "Barriers and Gateways to Communication," *Harvard Business Review* 30 (July 1952): 47.
10. Carl R. Rogers and Richard E. Farson, "Active Listening," in *Readings in Interpersonal and Organizational Communication,* eds. Richard Huseman, Cal M. Logue, and Dwight I. Freshley (Boston: Holbrooks Publishing Company, 1973, 2nd Edition), p. 541.
11. *Ibid.,* p. 550.
12. Charles M. Kelly, "Empathic Listening," in *Small Group Communication,* eds. Robert S. Cathcart and Larry A. Samovar (Dubuque, Iowa: William C. Brown Company, 1970), p. 253.
13. Ralph G. Nichols and Leonard A. Stevens, *Are You Listening?* (New York: McGraw-Hill Book Company, 1957), pp. 53–54.
14. Thomas Gordon, *Parent Effectiveness Training* (New York: New American Library, 1970), pp. 41–45.
15. Theodore H. Wright, "Learning to Listen: A Teacher's or a Student's Problem?" *Phi Delta Kappan* 52 (June 1971): 626.
16. Jack R. Gibb, "Defensive Communication," *Journal of Communication* 11 (September 1961): 142.
17. David Johnson, *Reaching Out* (Englewood Cliffs, New Jersey: Prentice-Hall, Inc., 1972), p. 47.
18. Lawrence M. Brammer, *The Helping Relationship* (Englewood Cliffs, New Jersey: Prentice-Hall, Inc., 1979), p. 73.
19. From *Active Listening Skills for Staff Development: A Cognitive Viewpoint* (St. Paul: Minnesota Department of Education), pp. 8–9.
20. Earl Koile, *Listening As a Way of Becoming* (Waco, Texas: Calibre Books, 1977), p. 91.
21. Loretta Girzaitis, *Listening a Response Ability* (Winona, Minnesota: St. Mary's Press, 1972), p. 42. Reprinted with permission.

concepts you will encounter

Critical Listening
Persuasion
Coercion
Motivated Sequence
Ethos / Source Credibility
Logos
Inductive Arguments
Deductive Arguments
Syllogisms
Enthymemes
Validity
Truth
Reasoning Fallacies
Hasty Generalizations
Causal Reasoning

Analogical Reasoning
Non Sequitur
Arguing in a Circle
Ignoring the Issue
Evidence
Testimonies
Facts / Opinions / Inferences
Rumors
Biases
Statistics
Pathos
Need Levels
Emotional Appeals
Emotive Language
Responsibilities

skills you should develop

Identifying the Dimensions of
    Source Credibility
Recognizing the Influence of
    Source Credibility
Evaluating Inductive Arguments
Evaluating Deductive Arguments
Detecting and Evaluating
    Reasoning Fallacies
Evaluating Evidence
Recognizing Need Levels
Identifying Emotional Appeals
Dealing Effectively with Emotive
    Language

critical listening

8

The fifth purpose for listening goes beyond comprehensive listening and adds the dimension of judgment to therapeutic listening, for critical listening is listening to comprehend and *then* evaluate the message. The critical listener makes a decision to accept or reject a message on the basis of sound criteria. Listening should be critical especially when the listener is exposed to a persuasive message—a message designed to influence a change in the listener.

The Need for Critical Listeners

Now, as never before, we are being confronted with speakers who want to change our behavior. Daily, we are flooded with persuasive messages—ranging from family members' pleas to buy that beach condominium or to vacation in Hawaii, campaign speeches, radio and television commercials, salespersons' pitches, and telephone solicitations to problem solving discussions, lobbyists' views, briefings advocating new procedures, and leaders' pleas. Hayakawa acknowledges the unparalleled position in which we are currently living:

> The citizen of today, Christian or Jew or Mohammedan, financier or farmhand, stockbroker or stockboy, has to interpret more words a day than the citizen of any earlier time in world history. Literate or semi-literate, we are assailed by words all day long: news commentators, soap operas, campaign speeches, newspapers, the propaganda of pressure groups or governments—all of these trying to tell us something, to manipulate our beliefs, whether about the kind of toothpaste to use or the kind of economic system to support.[1]

Since freedom of speech assures equal rights to both the honest and dishonest speaker, we must be effective critical listeners if we are to protect and control ourselves rather than allowing others to control us. Wendell Johnson has stressed the importance of our being critical listeners.

> As speakers, men have become schooled in the arts of persuasion, and without the counter-art of listening a man can be persuaded—even by his own words—to eat foods that ruin his liver, to abstain from killing flies, to vote away his right to vote, and to murder his fellows in the name of righteousness. The art of listening holds for us the desperate hope of withstanding the spreading ravages of commercial, nationalistic, and ideological persuasion.[2]

Our becoming schooled in the art of listening critically, then, as Gunn has stated, "may mean not just being realistic and alert to the times in which we are alive, but quite literally it may mean being and staying alive."[3]

As we have previously stated, the critical listener's decision to accept or reject a message must be based on sound criteria. Understanding the process of persuasion as it applies to listeners will aid the listener in establishing these criteria and making careful judgments when he or she is listening not only to so-called "informative" messages which are mere rumors but also to persuasive messages.

The concept of influence may be viewed in terms of a continuum of persuasion which has been defined by Goyer as "the process by means of which one party purposefully secures a voluntary change of behavior, mental and/or physical, on the part of another party by employing appeals to both feeling and intellect.[4] On the other hand, we have coercion in which the receiver is given no choice or a choice between highly undesirable alternatives.

If you are told to vote for Raymond Jones for the city mayor because he can accomplish his campaign promises, you are given a *persuasive* choice to accept or to reject the speaker's thesis. If you are told to stop smoking because you will die of lung cancer, you are presented with a more *coercive* message. The extreme of coercive influence is the use of force. A robber's message of "Hand over your money" at gunpoint is a graphic example of where you, the receiver, would be left with no choice or with a choice between highly undesirable alternatives.

Most messages do not fit neatly into the persuasive or coercive category but, instead, fall somewhere along the continuum between the two extremes. Thus, advertising propaganda, political campaigns, religion, education, and most means of social influence will share elements of persuasion and coercion. It is to be hoped, however, that these messages will ultimately be persuasive and, thus, leave listeners with a choice. The receivers' not being presented with a choice is inconsistent with a basic objective of American democracy—freedom of choice.

The process of influence usually takes the form of a psychological sequence. This sequence was identified by Monroe and has been labeled the "motivated sequence." According to Monroe, to persuade or to be persuaded, the message must conform to five basic steps:
1. Attention—getting the attention of the listener.
2. Need—demonstrating the problem, the need for the proposal.
3. Satisfaction—presenting the proposal to satisfy the need.
4. Visualization—illustrating what will happen if the proposal is accepted or what will happen if it is rejected.
5. Action—issuing a challenge or an appeal to the listener.[5]

These basic steps describe what occurs as we attempt to influence. It is a system, but it should be viewed as more of a process than the listing might suggest. Actually, some of the steps might transpire simultaneously. The results might be visualized, for instance, while the solution/satisfaction step is presented. Any persuasive message, however, whether it be an ad, a speech, or a sale's pitch, can be seen to conform to this psychological sequence.

Effective persuasion usually does not result in a change of behavior in the receiver on the basis of one persuasive message. A sequence of messages is required to accomplish the task. Thus, most persuasive efforts take the form of a campaign—television commercials, political campaigns, a series of speeches on an issue. When you consider the amount of stimuli bombarding us as receivers, it is understandable why a concerted effort over an extended period of time is necessary for meaningful change to result.

Skills Involved in Critical Listening

Given, then, that the persuasive sequence takes time and leaves the receiver with a voluntary choice, it is useful to consider the components of an effective persuasive effort. The classical Greek rhetorician, Aristotle, first described our system of persuasion in *The Rhetoric*. He determined that a persuasive message required three components: ethos, speaker credibility; logos, logical arguments; and pathos, psychological appeals. These three components must interact to be maximally effective in securing a voluntary change in the listener. As critical listeners, we need to be aware of how these components function to be persuasive.

While we can analyze a persuasive message according to these three components, we should note that listeners often are unable to distinguish the emotional from the logical components of a particular persuasive message. Some individuals may respond on an emotional level to a logical argument, while others may be more responsive on the cognitive level.[6] Individual listeners will respond differently to the same persuasive message.

Research on speaker credibility has been helpful in enabling us to identify some of the factors and dimensions of the concept. The three most frequently cited dimensions of source credibility are trustworthiness, expertness, and dynamism.[7] Most senders are perceived as possessing these dimensions in varying degrees; however, it certainly is possible for a sender to be perceived as having a high degree of all three of these relatively independent dimensions. The independent nature of these dimensions can be illustrated by the person who, while listening to a speaker, says to her friend, "He definitely doesn't know what he's talking about, nor does he look very honest, but he surely has charisma." Although there are probably additional factors that influence a listener's perception of a sender's believeability, current research indicates that trustworthiness, expertness, and dynamism are the three dimensions that are the most influential.

Skills Related to Ethos

Identifying the Dimensions of Source Credibility
It is difficult at this point to draw any hard and fast conclusions as to the extent to which a speaker's credibilty can influence us persuasively. Each listener will respond differently to the message source—before, during, and after the message presentation. The research does support the idea that there is some impact from

credibility. Andersen and Clevenger analyzed the data and drew these conclusions:

> The finding is almost universal that the ethos of the source is related in some way to the impact of the message. This generalization applies not only to political, social, religious, and economic issues but also to matters of aesthetic judgment and personal taste. Some evidence even shows that "prestige-suggestion" can affect the appetite for certain foods and can influence performance of perceptual and psychomotor tasks. On the other hand, there is not enough evidence to suggest that the amount of information gained from exposure to a message is related to the ethos of the source— at least this lack of relationship seems to be true of college populations. . . .
>
> Some auditors appear to be more susceptible to ethical appeal than others; some may be contra-suggestible. However, there is no evidence to show that suggestibility to prestige correlates well with intelligence, education, speech training, subject-matter competence, age, or sex. The only variable which seems clearly related to differences in suggestibility to prestige is the initial attitude toward the topic or the purpose: consistently, those who are neutral initially shift more often than do those who are at one extreme or the other.[8]

Recognizing the Influence of Source Credibility

The ethos of the source, as it does have some impact on the listener, operates even before the message is presented. Speaker credibility can influence the listener initially if the speaker has prestige, authority, and reputation with the listener. A well-known authority in his or her field, thus, will have considerable weight with the listeners even before the speaker begins to present his or her message. As listeners, we need to be aware of how we can be influenced by a person's past reputation and even by the person's reputation itself.

As listeners, we are also influenced by the profession of a speaker. In a February 1979, Harris poll, interviewers found that more than twice as many Americans had a great deal of confidence in television news, higher educational institutions, and medicine than they had in law firms, the White House, and organized labor.[9]

The speaker's credibility can be developed during the speech by what McCroskey has defined as "derived ethos." This credibility is enhanced through techniques the speaker utilizes to demonstrate his or her character, knowledge, and goodwill. Politicians citing biblical quotations, for example, illustrate the effort to demonstrate character. The speaker who discusses his or her own research and experiences with the topic will demonstrate the expertise of a credible speaker. The good will of a listener can be developed by the speaker demonstrating that he or she does have the best interests of the listener in mind as the speaker is advancing his or her proposal.

A good speaker will attempt to incorporate these techniques subtly rather than directly emphasizing that he or she is a credible speaker. The principle that operates in the listening process, essentially, is one of trustworthiness and belief. If we, as listeners, believe in the speaker, then it is easier for us to accept the speaker's message.

The extensive credibility crisis suffered by former President Richard M. Nixon represents the power of this component of persuasion. Ultimately, the American public, as receivers, was unable to accept any of his messages, so he found it necessary to step down from office. Jimmy Carter, campaigning for re-election as President in 1980, encountered similar credibility problems as Americans lost faith in his ability to control inflation or deal effectively with the taking of American diplomats as hostages in Iran.

We run the danger of being too persuaded by the credibility component. Political communicators, concerned with the "image" developed by candidates, recognize that often the image is what "sells" the candidate to the voting public. Joe McGinniss's *The Selling of the President 1968* details such efforts to "package" Nixon for the voters. McGinniss cites a memo from one of Nixon's image makers, Raymond K. Price:

> . . . we take the time and the money to experiment, in a controlled manner, with film and television techniques, with particular emphasis on pinpointing those *controlled* uses of the television medium that can *best* convey the *image* we want to get across. . . .[10]

As critical listeners, we should be aware of the influence of the image and not make our decisions solely on this basis.

Skills Related to Logos
The critical listener must also carefully examine the second persuasive component, logos—well-supported arguments that consist of both *true* propositions (or evidence) and *valid* relationships between all evidence presented and all conclusions reached. Basically, there are two argument structures with which the critical listener must be familiar: the inductive argument as traditionally studied is concerned with truth, and the deductive argument as traditionally studied is concerned with validity.

Evaluating Inductive Arguments
The inductive argument is the process of reasoning by which one arrives at a conclusion or generalization through examining specific, factual data of the same kind or class; it is reasoning from the specific to the general. In this type of reasoning, the speaker compares a number of instances to conclude that all other instances are the same.

For example, a teacher, citing past and present students who have studied and done well, may conclude that students who study receive high grades. From this observation, the teacher may reason inductively that all students who want to pass must study.

To determine the truth of an inductive argument, critical listeners should ask and answer the following questions:
1. Are the validating data true?
2. Are enough cases cited?

3. Are the cited instances representative of the whole being considered? Are they typical or atypical?
4. Is the class of persons, events, or instances about which the induction is made reasonably comparable in all relevant aspects?
5. Are there exceptions which do not lead to the expected conclusions? Are these exceptions accounted for?

Using these questions to evaluate the previously cited inductive argument, we see that the conclusion drawn by the teacher is not true. We all know students who do well in courses and yet do not study. In this case, other variables may not be accounted for in the argument: intelligence, aptitude, prior training, vocabulary, personality. We realize, too, that the number of specific examples suporting the conclusion must be sufficiently large to offset the probability of chance or coincidence; the critical listener demands many representative, specific instances before he or she will grant a general rule.

Evaluating Deductive Arguments

The second argument structure, the deductive (or syllogistic) structure, is the process of reasoning from a systematic arrangement of arguments consisting of a proposition stating a generalization (referred to as the major premise), a proposition stating a specific instance related to the generalization (the minor premise), and a conclusion which necessarily must follow from the premises. Deductive reasoning is reasoning from the general to the specific, and it infers that what is *presumed* true of all members of a class is true of some members of that class. The teacher might want to present his or her same argument deductively:

All students who want to pass must study.
You are a student who wants to pass.
Therefore, you must study.

To determine the truth of a deductive argument, the critical listener must ask and answer the following questions:

1. Is the generalization (major premise) universally true?
2. Does the specific item really belong to the general class?
3. Or, does the specific item represent an exception to the cited general class?

Most people do not talk in direct syllogisms. As listeners, we are confronted with truncated deductive arguments that Aristotle identified as enthymemes. Enthymemes are actually modified forms of syllogisms that have one or more of their premises or their conclusions omitted. They can operate effectively only if speaker and listener can share, mentally, the premise(s) or conclusion which the speaker does not state. If we are alert to their utilization, we can better analyze the speaker's argument for its validity.

The teacher, for example, who *assumes* that those in the class want to pass most likely would use an enthymeme rather than a direct syllogism. The teacher might say, "You'd better study for the exam." If the students (here the listeners) mentally share with the teacher (the speaker) the omitted premises that all

Figure 8.1.
Diagram of a valid enthymeme.

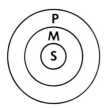

students who want to pass must study and that they are students who want to pass, the enthymeme can operate effectively.

When analyzing the validity of an enthymeme, the critical listener should first set up the enthymeme in the formal arrangement of a syllogism. For example, if a speaker states this enthymeme, "Mr. Jones voted for Jane Baker; he must be a proponent of the E.R.A.," the listener should immediately set up this syllogism:

Major Premise: All who voted for Jane Baker are proponents of the E.R.A.
Minor Premise: Mr. Jones voted for Jane Baker.
Conclusion: Therefore, Mr. Jones is a proponent of the E.R.A.

To help us visualize a syllogism, we can put the relationships into symbols:

Middle term$=$M
Subject of conclusion$=$S
Predicate of conclusion$=$P
All M (people who voted for Jane Baker) are P (proponents of the E.R.A.)
S (Mr. Jones) is an M (voter for Jane Baker)
S (Mr. Jones) is a P (proponent of E.R.A.)

We can also diagram the relationship between the propositions of a syllogism by using circles to represent the classes involved. The premises give us directions for the construction of the circles. In a valid argument, the directions compel the circles to show that the *conclusion is inescapable*. Let us examine the validity of the enthymeme above. The circles show that the conclusion is inescapable; thus, this enthymeme is valid.

At this point, we must more clearly differentiate between validity and truth. When we speak of validity, we have in mind the nature of the relationships between propositions rather than the truth of the propositions. We can tell by the construction of the syllogism if the argument is valid in itself. If the conclusion is forced by the premises, the argument is valid; if the conclusion does not necessarily follow, the the argument is not valid. We test the validity of an argument by *assuming* the premises true for the sake of argument and then observe if the conclusion must follow. Can a syllogism be valid while the premises are not true? Yes. If an argument is valid and the premises are true, is the

Figure 8.2.
Diagram of a valid syllogism.

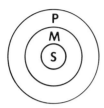

conclusion true? Yes. We must not confuse validity with truth. People too frequently are convinced of the truth of a proposition because they can see that it
logically follows from certain premises while they fail to notice that the premises
are not true. A sound argument, to repeat, depends on both *truth* and *validity*.

Previously, we evaluated the truthfulness of the teacher's syllogism, and we
assessed it as being false, but let us see if it is valid.

Major Premise: All students who want to pass must study.

Minor Premise: You are a student who wants to pass.

Conclusion: Therefore, you must study.

Symbolically, it would be as follows:

All M (students who want to pass) are P (students who must study).

S (You) are an M (student who wants to pass).

S (You) are a P (student who must study).

Yes, the syllogism is valid; however, because the argument does not have both
validity and truth, it is not sound.

To analyze more critically the validity of a syllogism, you must know what
conditions a valid syllogism must meet. The most important conditions are the
following:

1. There must be three terms, no more and no less.
2. Every term must be used twice, no more and no less.
3. A term must be used only once in any premise.
4. The middle term which *does not* appear in the conclusion must be *distributed*
   at least once. A term is distributed if the pattern of the statement indicates
   that the term refers to *all* (used in a universal sense) the members of a class
   designated by it; it is undistributed if the pattern does not indicate that the
   term refers to *all* (or *every* or *none*) but instead uses terms such as *some* or
   most. We must be cautious of omitted qualifiers where *all* is assumed (for
   instance, "rock stars use hard drugs.")
5. Any term that is distributed in the conclusion must be distributed at least
   once in the premises.
6. At least one of the premises must be affirmative. Only one negative premise
   may occur in any given syllogism.
7. At least one premise must be universal (distributed); only one particular
   (some, most) premise can occur in a given syllogism.

Figure 8.3.
Diagram of two valid syllogisms.

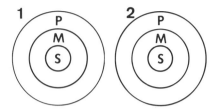

8. If one premise is negative, the conclusion must be negative.
9. If one of the premises is particular, the conclusion must be particular.
10. A particular subject (minor premise) may not be distributed (universal) in the conclusion.

Often, the use of the enthymeme will involve more than one formal syllogism; it may be polysyllogistic: "Any drug that can lead to addiction is evil, and, therefore, codeine should be made illegal." This enthymeme, put in the formal and symbolic pattern of two categorical syllogisms, would be as follows:

All M are P   1. Drugs that can lead to addiction are evil.
S is an M   Codeine is a drug that can lead to addiction.
S is P   Therefore, codeine is evil.
All M are P   2. That which is evil should be made illegal.
S is an M   Codeine is evil.
S is P   Therefore, codeine should be made illegal.

This is a valid argument.

As you have studied this material, you have probably wondered how you as a listener can possibly mentally convert enthymemes into formal syllogisms, draw circles, ask and answer the crucial questions, and determine the validity as well as the truth of the speaker's argument while the speaker continues to speak. We admit that these acts may be difficult to perform in the beginning, but developing an understanding of how to analyze logical arguments, concentrating intently, exerting physical and mental energy, capitalizing on the difference between speech speed and thought speed, asking questions whenever possible, and practicing will make you more effective critical listeners.

Detecting and Evaluating Reasoning Fallacies

As listeners, we cannot assume that all speakers present sound arguments. Too frequently, the speaker may use faulty reasoning—fallacious reasoning that allows a listener to draw from evidence a claim that is not justified. We must have the ability to recognize fallacies in reasoning so that we can reject the false claims advanced by some speakers.

Hasty Generalizations. We may be exposed more to the hasty generalization than to any other fallacy in oral discourse. This fallacy consists of the speaker drawing unwarranted, general conclusions from an insufficient number of cases (instances). A principal whose school has been vandalized by *some* long-haired youths might fall prey to the hasty generalization; at the next P.T.A. meeting, the principal may then condemn *all* long-haired youths as vandals and urge parents to restore law and order in the home. Such a hasty generalization is based on too few instances and does not account for many of the other variables which could be involved. In order to evaluate the hasty generalization, the critical listener should use the following questions:

1. Is there a sufficient number of cases cited to warrant the conclusion?
2. Is the generalization consistent with all known facts?
3. Is there an exception to the generalization?
4. Have negative instances been accounted for?
5. Are qualifiers (*some, few,* etc.) used?
6. Are the instances cited representative of the entire class? Have the instances been selected entirely at random?

Carefully evaluating hasty generalizations will prevent the critical listener from falling prey to the speakers who use them.

Faulty Causal Reasoning. Another fallacy involving generalizing is the faulty causal generalization. Some speakers, recognizing that other factors do contribute to the effect, speak of one event being *the cause* of another because it is the important difference; they mean it is the cause with a high degree of probability. Unfortunately, other speakers do not recognize that there are other contributing factors, and they argue that what *usually* (or *sometimes* or even *often*) happens *always* happens; instead of indicating that they recognize other contributing factors by saying "a common cause," "a frequent cause," "a prominent cause," "one cause," or "a probable cause," they use "the cause" without qualification, and, as a result, they make a faulty causal generalization. For example, Betty may say, "My allergy disappeared the day after I took Clogless. I certainly recommend the use of that medicine!" The speaker is alleging that Clogless was the *cause* of the disappearance of her allergy (effect).

Another type of faulty causal reasoning is *post hoc, ergo propter hoc* ("after this, therefore, because of this") reasoning. *Post hoc* reasoning is used by the speaker, who—without proof—supposes that because one event follows another event, the first is the cause of the second. An effect, granted, must follow a cause, but a prior event does not necessarily cause the event that follows. Craig, for instance, is using *post hoc* reasoning when he remarks, "I didn't make that big sale this afternoon because I walked under a ladder right before I met with Mr. Gwynn."

The critical listener, when listening to such faulty causal reasoning, should use the following questions in order to evaluate the reasoning:

1. What is the alleged cause?
2. What is the alleged effect?

3. Is the cause really capable of producing the effect?
4. Is the effect the result of a sequence of events or a coincidence of events?
5. Are there possibly other intervening causes?
6. Was the cause really operating? Have the alleged facts been verified?
7. When past experience is involved, has the alleged effect *always* followed the observed cause?
8. Does the alleged cause precede the alleged effect?

These questions—asked mentally or orally—can greatly assist the critical listener in uncovering faulty causal reasoning.

Faulty Analogical Reasoning. In addition to using faulty causal reasoning, speakers frequently use faulty analogical reasoning. An analogy is the assertion that cases which resemble each other in some respects will resemble each other in some other respects. Every analogy must break down at some point since no cases are identical. Speakers use faulty analogies when they assume (1) that shared properties will continue indefinitely and/or (2) that shared properties are similar in all aspects relevant to the issue being discussed, when in truth they are not. For example, Mary Beth tells her friend, "Leving Motors fixed my Chevy really well; it hasn't needed any additional repair work for three years. I bet Leving mechanics can correct the problems with your Mercedes just as well." Here the speaker is assuming that the shared properties (two cars and each—at one time—in need of repair) will continue indefinitely and that the shared properties are similar in all relevant aspects. The critical listener should immediately ask several questions. Does Leving Motors still exist? Does Leving Motors specialize only in repairing Chevrolets? Does Leving Motors also repair Mercedes Benzes? Is the repair work at Levings as good now as it was three years ago? Are the mechanics who repaired the Chevy still working at Leving Motors? Are the present mechanics equally qualified to repair both Chevrolets and Mercedes Benzes? Are parts as easily accessible for the Mercedes as for the Chevy? Is the type of repair work that the Mercedes needs the same as that which the Chevy once needed? The answers to these questions may indeed illustrate that the compared cases are not alike in all essential aspects.

To detect the faulty analogical reasoning of examples such as this one, the critical listener should ask and answer the following questions:

1. Are there significant points of similarity?
2. Are there enough resemblances to warrant a comparison?
3. Are the compared cases alike in all essential aspects?
4. Does the comparison overlook fundamental differences? Are the points of difference critical? Noncritical?
5. Is the analogous situation representative?
6. Do the points brought out really exist?
7. Are only literal analogies used as logical proof?

By using these questions when confronted with analogical reasoning, the critical listener will have one more means of controlling his or her own decision making.

Three of the many other common types of reasoning fallacies are *non sequitur*, arguing in a circle, and ducking or ignoring the issue. These, too, can be deceiving to the listener.

Non Sequitur. Translated literally, *non sequitur* means "it does not necessarily follow," and it is a general name for all irrelevancies. Although it is involved in all invalid syllogisms since they claim that a conclusion follows when it does not, the term is generally used to refer to the widely irrelevant conclusion.

A graphic example of the *non sequitur* is the argument critics advanced against the National Aeronautics and Space Administration's Apollo moon missions. Critics of the program argued that the money spent on the missions should be spent on earth for domestic needs. Such an argument did not follow because it assumed that the small N.A.S.A. budget would be reallocated to meaningful "earthly" causes while it overlooked the spin-off benefits of the space program to technology, medicine, and science throughout the world.

Arguing in a Circle. Another common fallacy is arguing in a circle. When using this fallacy, the speaker tries to prove a given statement with another statement that depends for its proof upon the first statement. The speaker who argues that the promises of Iran's Ayatollah Ruhollah Khomeini cannot be trusted because Khomeini does not keep his word is arguing in a circle; the "reason" that follows the word *because* is the same assertion that precedes *because*. Arguing in a circle can be seen in its height of absurdity in the following example: Living together without benefit of marriage is justified because living together without benefit of marriage is justified.

Ignoring the Issue. The third common reasoning fallacy is ducking or ignoring the issue. The speaker who uses this type of fallacy uses irrelevant arguments to cloud the real issue or argument. One of these irrelevant arguments is the *ad hominem* argument—attacking the personal character of the source of the statement rather than focusing on the content of the issue itself. George McGovern's first running mate in 1972, Senator Thomas Eagleton of Missouri, was the victim of this fallacy—character assassination. Rather than focus on his political record and proposals as a prospective vice-president, critics forced his resignation by concentrating on his former psychiatric record.

A second irrelevant argument is the *ad populum* argument—appealing to the people in terms of their prejudices and passions rather than focusing on the issues at hand. An example of this argument is the following: A woman is running for mayor of Laurel, Maryland; her opponent has been a resident of the city for only five years. In one of her campaign speeches, she states, "I was born in Laurel, and I have been a Laurelite all my life. I attended Laurel Elementary School, Laurel Junior High School, and Laurel Senior High School. Many of you were there when I missed that final desperation shot and our girls' basketball team lost that heartbreaking final game at the state tournament. And, many of you were there to share my happiness when I was crowned Laurel's Junior Miss. . . ."

The final form of ignoring the issue is the *ad ignoratiam* argument. The speaker who uses this argument attempts to prove that a statement is true (or false) because it cannot be disproved (or proved). Not being able to disprove a point is not the same as proving it; only concrete evidence can prove or disprove a statement. An example of this fallacy is the following: Since the opponents of the discipline policy cannot prove that detention has not improved discipline in the school, it follows that detention is an effective disciplinary measure.

These are just a few of the numerous reasoning fallacies that speakers intentionally and nonintentionally use. It is vital that critical listeners be aware of these fallacies as well as others if they wish to become more adept in evaluating speakers' arguments.

Evaluating Evidence

The effective critical listener will analyze the soundness of not only the speaker's argument but also the speaker's support—the evidence.[11] A speaker will support his or her assertions with any of a variety of types of evidence, including testimonies, facts, opinions, inferences, and statistics.

Regardless of the type of evidence the speaker uses, the listener can apply some tests to the evidence in order to assess its soundness. The listener should attempt to determine the *clarity* of the evidence (how clear and intelligible it is), the *accuracy* of the evidence (how true, precise, and correct it is), and the *reliability* of the evidence (how dependable, trustworthy, and credible it is).

This determination may be made through the application of some basic questions to the evidence:

1. Is the evidence clear?
2. Is the evidence consistent with other known evidence?
3. Is the evidence consistent with the speaker?
4. Is the evidence timely?
5. Is the evidence applicable to the argument?
6. Is the evidence pertinent to the argument?
7. Is the source of the evidence reliable?
8. Is the source of the evidence competent in the area in which he or she is being quoted?
9. Is the source of the evidence free to report all of his or her findings?
10. Is the source of the evidence sincere?

Detecting Fallacious Testimonies. Most of us are quite aware of the fallacious testimonies with which the advertising industry bombards us. Testimonies from famous models, movie stars, and sports stars endorsing products appeal to our sense of imitation, even though experts in the field would be in a better position to offer sound support. Thus, a carpet manufacturer will call on a glamorous model rather than a Ph.D. in textiles to sell the company's product. And we are all most likely familiar with the famous football hero who endorses items from popcorn poppers to panty hose. Unfortunately, many listeners pay no more attention to evaluating sources' credibility when they are listening to messages of grave concern than they do when they are listening to commercials.

Distinguishing among Facts, Opinions, and Inferences. In addition to evaluating testimonies, the crtcial listener must distinguish between statements of fact and statements of opinion. Although many of us believe that a fact is a fact and that there is nothing else to say about facts, too frequently speakers pass opinions off as facts (often introduced by words such as "It is said that . . .," "They say that . . .," "I heard that . . .," "It is a fact that . . .," etc.), and listeners do not challenge the accuracy and realiabilty of the speakers' so-called "facts." Whether or not speakers use facts or opinions to "prove" their assertions should be a crucial question for the critical listener, or he or she may become, as Windes and Hastings believe, what the American audience has become:

> . . . the American audience has become so accustomed to hidden persuasion, so victimized by the engineers of consent that it will accept the truth of assertions with virtually no proof except the authority of the advocate, whether . . . a news commentator, politician, or public figure, or . . . a commercial announcer.[12]

Facts are truths known to exist. They can be determined by direct observation and/or they can be verified by a reliable source. When we cannot directly observe facts, we obtain our facts through reliable sources "as to what the facts probably were, are, and will be."[13] Facts are open to anyone who wishes to investigage them, and they can stand independent of the sources who report them. However, since few of us—as listeners—can actually investigate the majority of the facts we listen to, it is increasingly important that we consider the credibility of the speakers who present them.

Opinions, on the other hand, are statements of personal judgments and preferences. Though open to dispute, opinions cannot be positively and objectively proved or disproved because they are expressions of their possessors' own perceptions. Although opinions cannot be tested for proof, they can be evaluated, and the critical listener should carefully examine whether or not the stated opinions are made by reliable sources who are speaking in their areas of competency.

In assessing the factual basis of speakers' message content, the critical listener must not accept inferential statements as statements of fact. Inferences are statements of interpretation. Sometimes directly stated and other times merely implied, inferences are speakers' guesses or conclusions about what is not known made on the basis of what is known, and frequently they are in the form of statements of prediction. Speakers may not—knowingly or unknowingly—identify their material so what is presented from their inferences may appear to be facts.

William V. Haney's famous uncritical inference test illustrates the inability of most of us to distinguish what is presented to us as fact, inference, or judgment (opinion). Haney suggests that we have difficulty but that ". . . one can learn to make this distinction habitually and thus markedly increase his 'inference-awareness.' "[14] As critical listeners, we must make this distinction and then base our acceptance or rejection of inferences on the evidence used to support them as well as on the credibility of the source.

Detecting Rumors. Another type of biased communication that can be especially troublesome to the uncritical listener is the rumor. In the classic study of rumor, Allport and Postman defined rumor as "a specific (or topical) proposition for belief, passed along from person to person, usually by word of mouth, without secure standards of evidence being presented."[15] The rumor frequently represents a magnified inference which becomes more distorted as it is transmitted from person to person. It may not be based on any factual data at all. *Newsweek* reported a costly rumor in Japan:

The $5 Million Rumor

December is bonus time in Japan, the season when banks are ordinarily swamped by yen-laden depositors. But at the Toyokawa Credit Association in Kozakai, a small industrial town 160 miles southwest of Tokyo, things didn't work out that way. In one wild 36-hour period last week, 5,000 people staged a run on the bank, withdrawing a staggering 1.4 billion yen—or $5,007,140.

What provoked the stampede was a rumor that the bank was going under. And with all Japan jittery these days because of the crippling Arab oil boycott, the government was determined to find the culprit. Eighty detectives were dispatched to Kozakai, and after a thorough investigation, police revealed that the originator of the rumor was a high-school girl, who, as a joke, had tried to discourage a friend from working at the bank by cracking: "You'd better be careful. You may not keep your job for long because that bank's in financial danger." The classmate repeated the remark to her aunt, who repeated it to a friend, who. . . .[16]

The critical listener will seek the evidence, verify the sources, and sort out the biases in the communication so that such problems as rumors are not perpetuated.

Detecting Biases of Chief Information Sources. A revealing discussion of biases of our chief sources of information—the press, the government, pressure groups, and professional scholars—is found in Newman and Newman's book, *Evidence.*[17] The critical listener would be wise to read this book to understand the bias with which information is transmitted.

Analyzing Statistical Data. The discerning listener also should read Huff's delightful *How to Lie with Statistics,* an eye-opening exposé of the misuses of statistical data.[18] Huff, a statistician, illustrates many distortions from statistical evidence and recommends that individuals ask five questions to test statistical evidence: Who says so? How does he know? What's missing? Did somebody change the subject? Does it make sense?[19] We suggest that the critical listener also use the following questions as guides in evaluating statistical evidence:

1. Who wants to prove what?
2. Do the statistics come from reliable and objective sources?
3. How were the statistics gathered?
4. Are the statistics based on an adequate and representative sample?
5. Do the statistics cover a sufficient period of time?
6. Are the units being compared actually comparable?
7. Are the statistics the most current available?

8. How were the data treated statistically?
9. What conclusion do the statistics support?
10. How relevant to the issue are the statistics?
11. Can the results be verified?
12. Are the statistics supported by other findings and other sources?

Obtaining the answers to these and other questions relevant to assessing statistical evidence will help the critical listener, as Huff suggests, "avoid learning a remarkable lot that isn't so."[20]

Skills Related to Pathos

Recognizing Need Levels

In addition to ethos and logos, the third key component of persuasion is pathos, the psychological appeals used by the speaker to gain emotional response from the listener. As humans, we respond at various need levels. Maslow suggests that we have five such levels.[21] At the first, most basic level are physiological needs— food, sleep, sex, drink, shelter. These needs must be satisfied before an individual can be motivated at a second level—the safety needs. Safety needs such as security, stability, protection, and strength are important motivators when any sort of threat to these needs might be present. The third level consists of the belongingness and love needs, our social motivators. Americans are highly motivated by this need to belong, as evidenced by our affiliations with many groups. The fourth need level is identified by Maslow as the esteem needs. These needs represent both self-esteem, our desire for achievement and mastery, and esteem of others, our desire for reputation and prestige. These needs spring from our belongingness needs and represent a further stage in accomplishing our goals. Finally, at the fifth level in the hierarchy, Maslow identifies the need for self-actualization, our desire for self-fulfillment. Maslow suggests that we may be striving for this if other needs have been met, but the self-actualized person probably does not exist.

An understanding of these need levels aids speakers in selecting message appeals which will best meet the needs we have as listeners. Skillful persuaders who wish to secure a change in our mental or physical behavior regarding some person, some belief, some product, some act, some policy, some philosophy can— by employing appeals to our needs—motivate us to indulge in our feelings rather than in our reasoning.

Identifying Emotional Appeals

If we, as critical listeners, know the appeals that are commonly used and can identify them as emotional appeals, we will be able to participate in communicative acts in a more rational manner. To aid us in maintaining our rationality and objectivity, we should ask ourselves these questions when we are confronted with emotional appeals:

1. What is the speaker's intent?
2. Is the speaker attempting to manipulate me?

Daily, we are flooded with emotional
appeals—appeals made on the
telephone, the radio, the
television. . . .
Photo by Robert Tocha.

3. Does the speaker have honest motives?
4. Who will benefit if the speaker's intent is achieved?
5. Does the speaker combine emotional appeal with reasoning (evidence)?
6. How am I responding?
7. Am I responding on a purely emotional level?
8. Am I allowing my emotional weaknesses to be exploited?

Utilizing these questions will assist us in understanding our responses to the numerous psychological appeals we receive. Among the emotional appeals that speakers employ are the following eighteen that Monroe has identified.[22]

Acquisition and Savings.   The speaker might appeal to our need for acquisition and saving by stressing how the proposal can save us money. Generally, everyone likes a bargain, especially in inflationary times, so a considerable amount of product advertising is based on this appeal.[23]

Adventure.   A second appeal is the appeal to adventure. The listener's desire to explore new worlds, see exciting things, and participate in different events is often stressed. Amusement and theme parks and travel agencies are two industries that rely heavily on our desire for adventure.

Companionship.   A third appeal, companionship, arouses in us the desire to be with other people. Have you ever noticed how advertisers seldom associate a product with just one person? Since we are motivated by companionship, motivational researchers have concluded that it would not be wise to associate products with loneliness. Appeals by organizations for membership will frequently stress the benefits of companionship with the organization.

Creativity. The appeal to creativity may be another motivator. Most of us enjoy expressing ourselves through some creative means such as decorating our homes, designing innovative products, or satisfying our artistic drives. The influence of this motivational force can be evidenced by the numerous arts and crafts shows and kits as well as the do-it-yourself manuals that are currently so popular.

Curiosity. An additional appeal is the appeal to curiosity. When our curiosity is aroused, we often respond by seeking answers to the *whys, whens, wheres, whos, whats,* and *hows* that we wish to investigate. Besides operating with our desire to know, the appeal to curiosity frequently operates with our desire for adventure, particularly if we are motivated to travel or explore new territory.

Destruction. Some speakers may attempt to use the appeal to destruction. This appeal calls for destruction of an existing rule, institution, etc. If the existing factor is depicted as a real problem, overthrow can be aroused. It is a difficult appeal to handle because it can be so destructive. The critical listener should be certain that the speaker has an alternative to put in place of what is to be destroyed. In the late 1960s, many students—as well as non-students—were vehemently calling for the overthrow of the entire institution of higher learning. What was missing in so many of the appeals to destruction, however, was any attempt to offer real alternatives to the existing structure of higher education.

Fear. The fear appeal, presenting a sense of threat to the receiver, attempts to motivate the receiver to act. Research in the fear appeal suggests that it may be possible for the speaker to overdo a fear appeal so that the listener may be even further strengthened in opposition of the stand. This strengthening of the opposing view is known as the "boomerang effect" and has shown up in several studies of the appeal. After reviewing research studies of the use of the fear appeal, Colburn recognized that it is difficult to genealize as to the effectiveness of the appeal since it will affect each individual receiver differently. He did note, however that "when fear-arousing appeals are used, speakers and writers will be more likely to gain acceptance of their recommendations if the strength of those appeals is proportionate to the importance of the issue in listeners' minds."[24]

Fighting. Closely allied to the appeal to destruction is the appeal to fighting. Prior to utilizing the destruction appeal, a speaker often employs the appeal to fighting by arousing the anger of his or her listeners. The appeal to fighting probably has more effect if it is used with a group of listeners rather than with one individual in an isolated setting. The speaker who asks, "Are you happy with your tax bills? Do you feel we've had enough?" is tapping the sense of anger in his or her taxpaying listeners.

Imitation. A less hostile appeal is that of imitation. This strongly motivates Americans, as evidenced by advertising appeals aimed at having us purchase cosmetics endorsed by famous Hollywood stars or shaving equipment used by great sports figures. In our attempts to "keep us with the Joneses," we demonstrate our drive to emulate others.

Independence. While our desire to emulate others is strong, a conflicting motivation may be our sense of independence. Some product advertisers have attempted to use this appeal to associate certain brands of cigarettes, for instance, with the independent cowboy alone on his horse or the liberated woman. Independence lies at the heart of our constitutional democracy, so it is inherent in American value systems. Wartime speakers, too, made considerable use of this appeal to mobilize public support for the war effort.

Loyalty. Keeping America independent also represents an appeal to loyalty. Loyalty to our nation, our friends and family, and our organizations is an important characteristic. The loyalty to nation, for example, represents patriotic appeals which continue to change. The "America—love it or leave it" movement polarized Americans so that some Americans no longer will respond to flag-waving patriotic appeals.

Personal Enjoyment. We are all highly motivated by personal enjoyment. Advertisers—recognizing that we long to fulfill our sensory and psychic desires for pleasures such as comfort, luxury, security, contentment, beauty, recreation, freedom, space, and sensory satisfaction—employ appeals to our experiences of present pleasures, our memories of past pleasures, and our anticipation of future pleasures. These appeals indicate how we are capable of responding on a higher order of Maslow's hierarchy. Thus, if our basic needs are met, we can turn to fulfilling needs of enjoyment and aesthetics.

Power and Authority. There are times when the speaker might want to appeal to the listener's sense of power and authority. Such a motivator could be appropriate in developing more responsibility in a group of administrators, for example. It is an appeal used in the auto industry to persuade buyers to purchase large engines. The appeal to power is also a strong motivator to mobilize a nation to wage war.[25]

Pride. Another powerful emotional appeal is the appeal to our sense of pride. Recognizing the motivational force of individual self-esteem, speakers frequently attempt to develop a positive self-concept in their listeners. Managers have relied on an appeal to pride in work well done in industry to motivate workers to accomplish rigorous production schedules. Motivational research reveals that job satisfaction frequently stems from factors intrinsic within the job itself.[26]

Reverence. Still another appeal is the appeal to reverence or worship. This can be seen through manifestations of hero worship—having deep admiration, for example, for sports stars, entertainers, or historical figures—or in religious behaviors.

Revulsion. A motivator which is inherent in all of us is revulsion. As a specific type of fear appeal, this appeal can be effective. A speaker illustrating the effects of water pollution, for example, may show photographs and cite statistics on the effects to motivate receivers to support legislation for clean water. Such an appeal, if not overdone, can accomplish an initial arousal to action.

Sexual Attraction. Found in a great deal of advertising is a more pleasant appeal: sexual attraction. The appeal connects the beautiful young woman with the automobile commercial or the handsome young man with hair care products.

While it is a motivator, it can be overdrawn if the appeal does not relate to the product or the issue under consideration.

Sympathy. A potent appeal is the appeal to sympathy. A speaker who depicts homeless children, mistreated elderly, or forgotten veterans can motivate us to give our time, money and talents. Political speakers like to use the appeal to gain support for their causes and for their own elections.

As we are, then, motivated by such appeals, it helps listeners to know why they are responding as they are if they can identify the specific type of appeal which the speaker is using for psychological effect. At the extreme, the speaker will use only emotional appeals as a persuasive device. Such an attempt may succeed in persuading listeners at the moment. Over a period of time, however, we tend to forget the impact of such appeals and are left with only the core of the argument from the message. If there is no logical argument, then the message probably will not have a long-lasting effect.

Dealing Effectively with Emotive Language

In addition to using emotional appeals to arouse the listeners, persuaders frequently employ emotive language—often in the forms of name-calling and labeling. Using terms intended to degrade the referent (whether it be a person, issue, party, event, etc.) and generalizing about a person, party, issue or event, on the basis of limited knowledge are methods that speakers use to influence listeners to accept their views. An opponent of a certain candidate, for example, uses name-calling when he or she remarks to a voter, "Don't vote for Menard; she's a radical," and a person who may have seen a long-haired male arrested on television uses labeling when he or she says to a neighbor, "You'd be insane to hire that Colson boy; he's just one of those long-haired freaks who only cause trouble."

As listeners, we tend to react in two ways to language that triggers emotional reactions in us. If the views expressed are congruent with our point of view, we accept—without question—what is said and are ruled by our feelings rather than by our minds. On the other hand, if the views expressed are incongruent with our point of view, we immediately reject what is said and exercise emotional censorship—become "deaf" to what we do not want to hear and again become ruled by our feelings. Both reactions are reactions that the critical listener should disclaim.

Critical listeners should attempt to reduce the impact that certain emotionally laden words have on them. They should first recognize their own biases toward certain emotive words, analyze why these words affect them as they do, and then attempt to view the words rationally. With this new awareness, listeners will be better able to deal with the words when they meet them in communicative situations. Dealing effectively with them consists of recognizing them for what they are—emotive words, maintaining self-control while listening to the remainder of the speaker's message, examining the speaker's message for evidence that proves or disproves the speaker's claim, asking the speaker to provide evidence to support his or her claim if the evidence has not been presented, and then accepting or rejecting the speaker's view on the basis of having made a rational decision rather than an emotional decision.

Responsibilities of the Critical Listener

Critical listeners respond to persuasive messages designed to voluntarily change attitudes and actions. Understanding how these messages incorporate speaker credibility, arguments, and emotional appeals can enable listeners to more systematically and soundly evaluate those messages in order to decide whether to accept or to reject the speaker's proposal. According to Charles Larson, the critical listener has two major responsibilities:

> First, he must watch himself as he is persuaded or as he is subject to persuasive appeals; second, he must find some way to systematize his awareness by applying carefully considered criteria to the appeals he processes, judging their relevance, their truth, and their applicability to him.[27]

Accepting these responsibilities may be the difference between our being uncritical listeners controlled by others and being critical listeners controlled by ourselves.

Summary

In this chapter, we have examined the need for critical listening—listening to comprehend and *then* evaluate—as it applies primarily to messages that are persuasive in intent. To assist the critical listener in understanding the process of persuasion and establishing criteria to be used as a basis for the listener's decision to accept or to reject a persuasive message, we have presented (1) a definition of persuasion, (2) a psychological sequence that the process of influence usually follows, and (3) a detailed explanation of how the three components of persuasion—ethos, logos, and pathos—function in the persuasive effort. Additionally, we have provided lists of questions that the critical listener should ask and answer when he or she is evaluating various aspects of these three components. Lastly, we have discussed the following critical listening skills that the critical listener must develop in order for him or her to more systematically and soundly evaluate persuasive messages: identifying the dimensions of source credibility; recognizing the possible influence that source credibility may have on the listener; analyzing inductive and deductive argument structures to determine their truth and validity; detecting and evaluating reasoning fallacies; judging the clarity, accuracy, and reliability of evidence; recognizing need levels; and identifying psychological appeals and emotive language and recognizing their effects on the listener. The critical listener who develops these skills will have a sound basis upon which to evaluate persuasive messages and should have control over his or her decision making.

Activities to Try

1. Identify at least three radio and television commercials that utilize Monroe's Motivated Sequence. Then, present a detailed description (orally or in writing) of how each commercial uses each of the five basic steps.
2. Create your own examples of inductive arguments and read them to the class; the class will assess the truthfulness of the arguments.
3. Create your own enthymemes, put the relationships into symbols, diagram the relationships by using circles, read the enthymemes to the other members of the class, and have the class determine the validity and truth of the enthymemes.
4. Identify other conjunctions besides *because* that imply causal relationships. Examine your own written papers to see what causal terms you have used and to see if your causal reasoning is sound.
5. Bring in examples of logical fallacies found in various forms of communication (speeches, commercials, editorials, etc.). Share the examples with the class.
6. Identify five radio or television commercials that utilize fallacious testimonies. Then, orally describe each product being endorsed, the person doing the endorsing, and the name, title, or field of a person who would present a credible testimony.
7. Compile a list of special interest groups (religious, racial, political, professional, sexual, economic, etc.). Then, locate three or four statements of fact, opinion, and inference in articles that express the views of special interest groups. Each student will read each of his or her statements, and students will determine what type of statement (fact, opinion, or inference) is being read. When an opinion is stated, students will try to determine why that opinion is held by a particular special interest group.
8. Carefully note several opinions that your other instructors state. Then, privately meet with one instructor and find out why the instructor holds a particular opinion.
9. Find examples of statistics in the various medias and share the examples with the class. Students will critically evaluate the soundness of the examples.
10. Identify words or phrases that emotionally upset you. Then, share these words with the class, analyze why these words have such emotional impact, and try to eliminate conditioned reactions to these words.
11. List examples of emotional appeals and emotive words with which you are confronted over the next few days. Do not rely heavily on commercials. Then, share these examples with the class at the next class session.

Notes

1. S. I. Hayakawa, "The Task of the Listener," *ETC* 7 (Autumn 1949): 9–10.
2. Wendell Johnson, "Do We Know How to Listen?" *ETC* 7 (Autumn 1949): 3.
3. M. Agnella Gunn, "Background Preparation for the Role of Today's Teacher of English," paper presented at the Annual Convention of the National Council of Teachers of English, Chicago, Illinois, 1960.
4. Robert Goyer, class notes, Purdue University, 1965.
5. Alan H. Monroe and Douglas Ehninger, *Principles and Types of Speech,* 7th ed. (Glenview, Illinois: Scott Foresman and Company, 1974), pp. 353–380.
6. See, for example, Stanley F. Paulson, "Social Values and Experimental Research in Speech," *Western Speech Communication* 26 (Summer 1962): 133–139.
7. For a discussion of the dimensions of source credibility, see James C. McCroskey, *An Introduction to Rhetorical Communication* (Englewood Cliffs, New Jersey: Prentice-Hall, Inc., 1972), chapter 4.
8. Kenneth E. Andersen and Theodore Clevenger, Jr., "A Summary of Experimental Research in Ethos," *Speech Monographs* 30 (June 1963): 77.
9. Louis Harris, "Confidence in Most Institutions Down," ABC News—Harris Survey, I, 27 (March 5, 1979).
10. Joe McGinniss, *The Selling of the President 1968* (New York: Trident Books, 1969), p. 38.
11. The real impact of evidence in persuasive discourse may be disputed. After analyzing experimental research studies on the use of evidence, McCroskey drew conclusions which suggest that listeners may not be responsive to a speaker's evidence:
    1. Including good evidence has little, if any, impact on immediate audience attitude change or source credibility if the source of the message is initially perceived to be high-credible.
    2. Including good evidence has little, if any, impact on immediate audience attitude change if the message is delivered poorly.
    3. Including good evidence has little, if any, impact on immediate audience attitude change or source credibility if the audience is familiar with the evidence prior to exposure to the source's message.
    4. Including good evidence may significantly increase immediate audience attitude change and source credibility when the source is initially perceived to be moderate-to-low credible, when the message is well delivered, and when the audience has little or no prior familiarity with the evidence included or similar evidence.
    5. Including good evidence may significantly increase sustained audience attitude change regardless of the source's initial credibility, the quality of the delivery of the message, or the medium by which the message is transmitted.
    6. The medium of transmission of a message has little, if any, effect on the functioning of evidence in persuasive communication.

    See James C. McCroskey, "A Summary of Experimental Research on the Effects of Evidence in Persuasive Communication," *The Quarterly Journal of Speech* 55 (April 1969): 169–176.
12. Russel R. Windes and Arthur Hastings, *Argumentation and Advocacy* (New York: Random House, 1965), p. 96.
13. *Ibid.,* p. 99.

14. William V. Haney, *Communication Patterns and Incidents* (Homewood, Illinois: Richard D. Irwin, Inc., 1960), p. 21.

15. Gordon Allport and Leon Postman, *The Psychology of Rumor* (New York: Holt, Rinehart and Winston, Inc., 1947), p. ix.

16. "The $5 Million Rumor," *Newsweek,* 31 December 1973, p. 19. Reprinted by permission of the publisher.

17. Robert P. Newman and Dale R. Newman, *Evidence* (Boston: Houghton Mifflin Company, 1969).

18. Darrell Huff, *How to Lie with Statistics* (New York: W. W. Norton and Company, 1954).

19. *Ibid.,* pp. 122–142.

20. *Ibid.,* p. 122.

21. Abraham Maslow, *Motivation and Personality* (New York: Harper and Row, Publishers, 1970), pp. 35–58.

22. Monroe and Ehninger, *Principles and Types of Speech,* pp. 270–282.

23. For a scholarly treatment of motivational research and its application in the advertising industry, see James F. Engel, David T. Kollat, and Roger D. Blackwell, *Consumer Behavior* (New York: Holt, Rinehart and Winston, 1973).

24. C. William Colburn, "Fear-Arousing Appeals," in *Speech Communication Analysis and Readings,* eds. Howard H. Martin and Kenneth E. Andersen (Boston: Allyn and Bacon, 1968), pp. 214–223.

25. For a current discussion of this appeal, see David C. McClelland, "Love and Power: The Psychological Signals of War," *Psychology Today* 8 (January 1975): 44–48.

26. For a review of the research, see T. O. Jacobs, *Leadership and Exchange in Formal Organizations* (Alexandria, Virginia: Human Resources Research Organization, 1971), pp. 122–154.

27. Charles U. Larson, *Persuasion: Reception and Responsibility* (Belmont, California: Wadsworth Publishing Company, 1973), p. 13.

concepts you will encounter

Informal Listening
Television Perceptions
Formal Listening
Interview Question Schedules
Small Group Maintenance and
    Task Functions
Hidden Agenda
Decision-Making Agenda
Social Facilitation
Polarization
Circular Response
Pedestrian, Passive, Selected,
    Concerted, and Organized
    Audiences

listening roles

As listeners, we function in different roles depending upon the setting and the situation in which we are placed. We function informally in casual conversation and in many individual appreciative listening situations (e.g., listening to the radio). More formally, we listen in interviews, in small group discussions, and in public audiences. The distinction between formal and informal listening roles is a matter of context—whether we are in a structured communication situation or in a more relaxed setting.

Informal Roles

Conversation

Listening in casual conversation requires attention, concentration, and—importantly—the willingness to listen.

Frequently, conversation patterns for most of us can be characterized as *non-listening*. These characteristics, while important to casual listening, unfortunately may not be all that representative of our behaviors in most conversations.

Instead of listening, many of us anticipate what the person will say and just eagerly await our "turn" to chime in with our own tale.

> Janet: "And then she said she was sure I had strep throat and that I'd better. . . ."
>
> Mary: "Oh yes, I had strep throat once. I was put on penicillin, and it cleared up very fast. But I certainly was sick until. . . ."
>
> Janet: "Yes, it certainly is miserable. I remember looking at the little white spots in my throat and wondering. . . ."
>
> Mary: "Well, my throat was very red, and all my muscles ached, and I. . . ."
>
> Janet: "I heard that Larry went to Denver yesterday. . . ."

And on it goes. We need to be careful not to fall into this conversation trap of not listening.

In a very interesting book entitled *Egospeak,* Addeo and Burger describe this problem of not listening in conversations:

> The reason that no one listens, usually, is that our egos get in the way, in the sense that we're mentally formulating what *we're* going to say when the other person gets through speaking. Instead of digesting the other person's information, we are most often busy thinking only of how best we can *impress* him with our next statement. The result is what we call EgoSpeak.[1]

Some people who are recognized as great conversationalists may not be as talkative as the image suggests. Indeed, they may be attentive listeners who really say very little in a conversation. Persons in international affairs often note the differences between British and American conversation patterns. Britons, who are noted throughout the world as conversationalists, offer verbal responses to their conversation patterns. Americans, on the other hand, tend to rely on "uh huh" and nodding the head responses. Partners of attentive, responsive listeners tend to leave the conversation feeling good about the experience and grateful for the chance to have had someone with whom to converse.

Radio-Television
In addition to conversation, we are informal listeners as receivers of television and radio programming.

The popularity of mass media today suggests that we spend a great deal of our waking time as listeners—attending to radio and television broadcasts. In their infancy, both radio and television were much more oriented to larger audiences. Because only a few people could afford receivers, entire extended families or even communities would come together in the home of the fortunate radio or television set owner for an evening of listening. Indeed, in some less-developed countries, these gatherings are still common. Preparing television commercials for South American television, for instance, requires a "broader" approach, aimed to larger audiences in homes.

In America, however, we usually are "isolated" listeners so that radio and television have become very intimate media. Going to and from work, we listen to the radio in our cars on the expressway. Frequently, we have more than one television set in a home, so we are alone as viewers.

Radio, of course, relies solely on sound to project images. So we let radio listening "happen" to us through our auditory channels. In its heyday of popularity, radio became a very creative instrument for American culture and entertainment. Such popular shows as "The Shadow" and "Amos and Andy" reflected the effort by broadcasters to develop the medium in order to spark the imagination of the listener. Through vocal inflections and through sound effects, the listener was involved in the experience and, with concentration, could become a true participant in the event.

Radio, today, reflects some effort to return to its creative works. Some stations are willing to do more than broadcast the "Top 40" records and commercials with, perhaps, five minutes of news every hour. Radio drama has been revived, and even commercials have become more creative. Commercials for Blue Nun wine, for instance, involve clever scenarios by comics Anne Meara and Jerry Stiller. *Business Week* reports that revenue for sale of radio advertising spots will increase 15.3 percent in 1980, more of an increase than for television or magazine or newspaper advertising.[2]

Television, on the other hand is designed to be more of a video medium. We look at the screen and watch the action. Tony Schwartz, the famous media specialist, argues, however, that television is more auditory than we think. He recommends an experiment—turn out the picture and listen to the sound. He suggests that we would be impressed with how much, like radio, the television audio portion does involve us as listeners.[3]

In its infancy in the 1940s and 1950s, television relied on live productions in which anything could—and did—happen. Viewing television as an entertainment medium, producers attempted to offer live theatre (such as *Studio One* and *Philco Playhouse*) on a regular, consistent schedule. Today, however, the commercial television industry is very much geared to the presentation of lightweight situation comedies, afternoon soap operas, adventure shows, and news shows. Public television has attempted to cut through some of the deficiencies of such programming by offering such outstanding children's shows as *Sesame Street* and a wide array of educational and public affairs programs.

Despite some advances in educational television, one major concern about American television viewing habits is the effect that television portrayal has on us as individual viewers. The Federal Communication Commission and the Federal Trade Commission have studied the impact of advertising on children, and several agencies are concerned about the impact of televised violence on both children and adults. This impact was dramatized in August 1977, when a 15-year-old, Ronald Zamora, and a 14-year-old, Darrell Agrella, of Miami, Florida, were accused of fatally wounding an elderly neighbor with her gun while stealing $415 and her car. Zamora's attorney claimed that his continuous diet of violent crime shows on television was responsible for his behavior. Indeed, Zamora told the court that he had been influenced by a "Kojak" television program in designing his crime. He was convicted of murder and sentenced to life imprisonment.

George Gerbner and his colleagues at the Annenberg School of Communications in Philadelphia have conducted studies of violence on television and have devised "Violence Profiles" to demonstrate the amount of violence depicted on television. The 1979 study revealed that "in prime time, 70 percent of all programs still contained violence."[4]

Gerbner and his colleagues stress that television has become a powerful medium, dominating our lives from infancy on:

> The television set has become a key member of the family, the one who tells most of the stories most of the time. Its massive flow of stories showing what things are, how things work, and what to do about them has become the common socializer of our times. These stories form a coherent if mythical "world" in every home.[5]

As television shapes our perceptions of the world, it is interesting to note that the stories presented on television shows primarily are written and produced in Los Angeles. In an interesting book analyzing the influence of Los Angeles on television, Ben Stein argues that the view of society depicted on these adventure shows and on situation comedies is distorted. What we see is perhaps not representative of the other geographical regions of the United States.[6]

Since we tend to be "isolated" listeners with radio and television, our responses are much like those described as appreciative listening. Our individual tastes, standards, and interests will structure what we attend to as entertainment in the media. It should be recognized, however, that Americans turn to the television news shows as the major source of news. We have come to place great faith in the medium as our primary source of information about current events.[7]

Even though we rely so heavily on television for news and for entertainment, how efficient are we as television listeners? In a recent study conducted by Jacob Jacoby, a consumer psychologist, 2700 viewers in 12 geographic areas were asked questions about televised segments that they were shown. It is significant to note that the vast majority of the viewers in this study—more than 90 percent—misunderstood some part of what they saw. The range of misunderstanding was between one-fourth and one-third of any type of broadcast, though viewers were less likely to misunderstand commercials than entertainment or news programs. Jacoby argues, however, that the television listener brings to each viewing his or her past experiences and mental frame of reference as a means of interpreting and misinterpreting the messages. "Given that it is not possible to eradicate either the influence of past experience or the individual's current mental set, it may well be impossible to eradicate miscomprehension."[8]

Because we are typically so isolated as listeners of radio and television, we usually are informal listeners. As informal listeners, we frequently only partially attend to a broadcast; we often work at other tasks or even carry on conversations while the radio or television plays. Thus, we often miscomprehend radio and television messages. It is apparent that concentration, attention, and a willingness to listen could enable us to function more competently as listeners to radio and television.

Formal Roles

Interviews

On a more formal level, we listen in interviews. An interview may be characterized as conversation with purpose. The purpose may be to gather information, to advocate a position, to determine a policy, to solve a problem, or to provide a therapeutic experience.

To achieve its purpose, a good interview is carefully structured with an opening designed to establish rapport between the interviewer and the interviewee and to clarify the purpose of the interview. This step is necessary to develop an open communication climate, one in which both individuals feel comfortable as communicators.

The body of the interview, then, consists of the questions and responses, the heart of the interview itself. The questions, selected as to the purpose of the interview, may be as follows:

—open, designed for permitting a variety of responses ("Could you tell me how you happened to become interested in a career in broadcasting?")

—closed, designed to focus a particular response ("Do you feel that the present American foreign policy needs reassessment?")

—probe, designed to explore in greater depth ("You indicate that you feel we need to establish more substantial energy conservation measures. Could you tell me why you feel that way?")

—mirroring, designed to reflect back what the person has said in order to get him or her to continue talking. This is particularly useful in therapeutic listening. ("You don't feel your study habits are working very well?")

—leading, designed to specify a response, usually the response you want to hear. This form can be manipulative, particularly if it becomes a "loaded" question. ("You don't really want to continue this process, do you?")

A good interviewer uses a variety of these question types and prepares a short "schedule" of questions in advance so that the interview will take some focus and allow the interviewer and interviewee to accomplish their objectives within the specified time frame. A schedule of questions might take the form of a "funnel" going from more general questions to more specific ones. This form may be particularly helpful in information gathering interviews where you want to explore any of a number of directions in getting the information. An "inverted funnel" schedule, on the other hand, leads from specific to more general questions. It is useful in a problem-solving interview, for instance, where you might initially identify the specific problem and then pursue various, generalized solutions to that problem.

Whatever the schedule, the interviewer should recognize that it is designed to serve just as a *general* guide for the interview. The good interviewer will *adapt* to the interviewee and, if necessary, follow the interviewee's direction of thought in an interview if that train of thought will serve to accomplish the intended purpose just as well as the original plan. The interviewee should listen carefully to the questions asked and respond appropriately. As a general rule, it is most effective to stay within the line of questioning offered by the interviewer. If you have additional information, however, of if you feel that a different direction may more efficiently accomplish the objective of the interview, you might try moving beyond the schedule of questions that the interviewer has prepared. Some of the most effective interviews are those which are spontaneous, offering a true give and take between the two interview communicators.

In the closing of the interview, it is appropriate to use time to explore any further concerns, any unclarified points, or any last questions the interviewee may have. Also, it is wise to sum up what has been accomplished in the interview and, if needed, specify the next step to be taken so that both the interviewer and the interviewee know what to expect as an outcome of the communication.

While attention and responsiveness are keys to effective listening in an interview, there are barriers to listening effectiveness for which the interview listener should be on the lookout. Downs, Smeyak, and Martin identify these barriers as the tendency to evaluate, the tendency to be impulsive, the tendency to never respond, the tendency to use irritated nonverbal habits (e.g., avoiding eye contact, looking at your watch, doodling), and the tendency to allow interruption (either in person or by telephone).[9]

The key to effective listening in interviewing, then, is to listen carefully. Concentrate on what the other person is saying and then adapt your responses accordingly. The interviewer must listen in order to pursue the train of thought with meaningful questions. And the interviewee must listen in order to understand the questions and to provide the appropriate responses. Since both persons must adapt to each other, listening becomes the central core of communication in an interview.

Small Group Discussions

Many of the principles of effective listening in the interview apply as well to listening in small group discussions. Since a small group discussion typically involves five to seven people, each individual will spend the majority of his or her time engaged in listening. S. I. Hayakawa notes the importance of listening in discussions and conferences: "If a conference is to result in the exchange of ideas, we need to pay particular heed to our listening habits."[10] It is a process of careful listening and then adapting remarks to the general thrust of the content of the discussion.

Group discussions are characterized by maintenance and task functions. Individuals in groups perform these functions through the roles that they assume during the course of the group deliberation.

Maintenance functions refer to the interpersonal needs of the group—the human interaction itself. A group proceeds through the stages much like two people in an interpersonal relationship, and it is helpful to recognize these stages and listen to (and be sensitive to) the interpersonal needs of the group members during these stages.

The formation stage involves the building of rapport and opening of the channels of communication through careful listening among the members of the group. Once the group has come together and established a communication base, it frequently is necessary to break down conflicts that may occur among members. Various people in a group may clash on issues or even procedures, so much conflicts must be resolved before members will feel comfortable communicating with each other.

Resolution of conflict in a group may extend to the breaking down of "hidden agenda"—individual objectives which may not necessarily be compatible with the overall purpose of the group. A person may enter a group, for instance, to build a power base in order to assume a position of dominance. If assuming power is the true, but hidden, agenda of this individual, such an objective may work at cross purposes with the needs of the group. All persons must listen carefully in order to recognize areas of conflict and work to overcome them.

Once a communication bond has been established, however, a group will build cohesion, insuring that individuals do feel a sense of commitment to the group and to each other as members of that group. The development of cohesion—belongingness—in a group can be implemented through reinforcement. A group member who does actively participate as a listener as well as a speaker in the group and who is reinforced for that participation will feel good about belonging to the group. Throughout the discussion, sensitivity to the maintenance needs of the individual members and to the group as a whole requires each person to listen and respond appropriately.

In addition to these maintenance functions, the sensitive discussion participant will be an active listener in order to accomplish the task functions of the group. The task functions—getting the job done—will depend upon the purpose of the group discussion.

The group may come together for social purposes, in which case participants probably will engage in general conversation and thus participate as active informal listeners. As we have noted, effective listening in conversations requires attention, concentration, and a willingness to listen.

A group may have a therapeutic purpose, in which case the objective of the group is to permit each person an opportunity to express his or her feelings, frustrations, concerns. A successful therapeutic group depends very much on a warm, supportive climate. Each participant, thus, should apply the principles of therapeutic listening and build an atmosphere of trust so that individuals can express themselves with minimum risk.

A third discussion purpose is that of information sharing. Like information-sharing interviews, these discussions should be characterized by careful distinction between facts and opinions so that the information presented will be accurate and authoritative. All members of the group should research thoroughly in preparation for participation in the discussion. This research base is helpful to the careful understanding of the information presented by the various group members. Through active listening, the participant can adapt remarks to those made by previous participants and, likewise, gain a complete perspective on the information presented.

A decision-making discussion, on the other hand, requires participants to listen with understanding to the information presented and then to evaluate the ideas in order to arrive at a good solution. Most decision-making groups structure their agenda to follow a series of problem-solving steps similar to those suggested by John Dewey in *How We Think:*
1. Locating and defining the problem.
2. Exploring the problem.
3. Suggesting solutions.
4. Evaluating the solutions.
5. Choosing the best solutions.[11]

The key to effective implementation of Dewey's format is to explore the causes and effects of the problem thoroughly (essentially an information-sharing discussion) before moving on to the deliberation of how to solve the problem. Again, careful listening and adaptation are the keys to this process. While participants will have their own ideas about how to solve the problem, it is important that participants be willing to listen to other points of view and to accept different points of view if they are valid.

Bormann and Bormann note that effective listening in task-oriented groups requires that you be willing to be a message receiver when it is appropriate to

listen, to know the basic skills of listening as communication, and to practice and apply effective feedback techniques.[12]

In one of the few works written specifically about listening in group discussions, Kelly argues that we tend to think we should listen critically to messages in group discussion. He suggests that this tendency to critical listening interferes with understanding the message and that we should concentrate on listening empathetically in discussions. Kelly makes these recommendations for the discussion listener:

Remember the characteristics of the poor listener.

Make a firm initial commitment to listen.

Get physically and mentally ready to listen.

Concentrate on the other person as a communicator.

Give the person a full hearing.

Use analytical skills as supplements to, not instead of, listening.[13]

It should be evident that the accomplishment of the task and maintenance functions in a group discussion depend, to a very great extent, upon the listening skills of all of the participants. These listening skills may extend to the assumption of leadership roles as well. A person may assume a position of leadership in a group at a particular time in order to facilitate task and/or maintenance needs of the group. In some groups, one individual will maintain the role of leader throughout a discussion while, more typically, two or three people may share leadership functions. One person, for instance, might work to keep the group organized—on the agenda—while another person might work to bring the group members to closure in their discussion of various issues. Just as individual participants, then, must be careful listeners in a discussion, so too should those individuals who assume roles of leadership listen actively. Since small group discussions involve a number of people, the majority of each person's time will be spent in active listening. The accomplishment of the group's objectives will depend, then, on each person assuming the listening roles seriously.

Public Audiences

Just as active listening is important in the interview and in the group discussion, active listening is crucial to effectiveness in public listening. The individual who joins an audience to listen to a public speech should be able to concentrate all of his or her time, energy, and attention on the speech itself. Much of Ralph Nichols's research on listening comprehension deals with listening to lectures and speeches, so his advice to concentrate is especially useful. The principles of listening comprehension are pertinent if the speech is informative or inspirational. If the speaker is attempting to persuade the audience, then critical listening techniques will also be necessary. These techniques have been detailed in previous chapters.

The theatre/concert listener, on the other hand, usually is listening for appreciation. Consequently, our suggestions for gaining greater appreciation from a listening experience may be helpful. Whether one is a pubic listener for a speech or for a theatrical/musical event, it is helpful to recognize that we become part of an audience through a rather systematic process.

The process of becoming a listener in a public event is not accidental. The process is designed to help you get involved in the event. One element in this carefully-constructed process is what is known as "social facilitation." You are seated next to other people so that their responses (laughter, applause, silence) can affect—facilitate—how you will respond. You lose some of your self-identity and become part of the audience, perhaps laughing at a speaker's joke which, at home alone with the television set or radio, you would not find funny at all.

Another dimension of the audience process is known as polarization. The lights go down, and all attention is focused, then, on the actors on the stage. You cease your official interaction with those next to you (unless you continue to chat during the overture or have to get up for latecomers). This polarizing of attention further serves your willingness to "let go" and concentrate on the production, while you lose some of your own concerns and attitudes in the transformation.

An audience also functions through the process of a "circular response." The responses you give to speakers, actors, musicians (through your applause, laughter, even coughing and distractions) communicate to them. They, in turn, work to project the ideas, emotions, dialogue, lyrics, or dances to you and adapt as necessary to the response levels of the people in the audience.

The response you give to a production ultimately takes you back to your individuality. *Your* standards and values will structure your responses, so your reactions may differ from those of other people in the same audience. The more likely the audience will be homogeneous (sharing similar backgrounds, purpose), the more likely the response of the listeners will be similar and predictable.

Herbert Kupferberg, writing about the concert audience, notes that audience behavior often offers "perplexities and paradoxes." Concert season subscribers loyally pass down their tickets from generation to generation within a family, yet they will complain loudly about an orchestra's programs or policies. Leopold Stokowski, the famous conductor, was noted for his scoldings of Friday matinee subscription holders, "especially when they coughed, sneezed or rustled during his performance."[14]

While Stokowski's matinee audiences may not be typical, Hollingworth (in a classic study on the audience) identified five types of audiences that speakers may confront.[15] The pedestrian, casual, audience reflects the least amount of attention. Shoppers who stop to watch a demonstration of omelet making in a shopping center, for instance, would be a pedestrian audience. A passive audience, on the other hand, typically consists of captive listeners, much like those found in a classroom of students required to take a course. A more specific type of audience is the selected audience, consisting of individuals who have come together for a unified purpose (attending a civic association meeting on neighborhood safety, for example). The concerted audience is even more organized in its purpose, as the individuals probably have some direct "stake" in the outcome. The audience at a political rally, for instance, would be a concerted audience. At the most organized level, then, is the organized audience with complete orientation to the speaker. A military drill team, for example, would be an organized audience, completely controlled by the speaker.

Regardless of the orientation, effective communicators are prepared to anticipate the responses of the listeners in a public audience and to deal with those responses effectively. Paul Holtzman, for example, has drawn up a checklist of forty-four audience/listener factors which a speaker should analyze in preparation for communicating with a group. The analysis encompasses speaker-image factors, motivational factors, environmental factors, group-membership factors, and cognitive (listener knowledge and beliefs) factors.[16] A speaker who antici-

	Conversation	Radio / Television
Appreciative	Attention Concentration Sensitivity	Attention Concentration Sensitivity
Discriminative	Attention Concentration Sensory Acuity	Attention Concentration Sensory Acuity
Comprehensive	Attention Concentration Understanding	Attention Concentration Understanding
Therapeutic	Attention Concentration Understanding Empathy	Attention Concentration Understanding Empathy
Critical	Attention Concentration Understanding Evaluation	Attention Concentration Understanding Evaluation

pates a hostile reaction to his or her proposal from the listeners, for instance, should be prepared with arguments which may "disarm" the audience and sway them toward the speaker's point of view. And as listeners, we should be willing to listen to the entire presentation before forming judgments about it, allowing the speaker the chance to explain his or her point of view.

The various listening roles that we assume in communication contexts certainly do overlap the various types of listening that we do. We may set different listening objectives for different listening situations. This concept might be illustrated by a grid:

	Conversation	Radio/ Television	Interview	Small Group	Public Speech	Theatre/ Concert
Appreciative						
Discriminative						
Comprehensive						
Therapeutic						
Critical						

The concept might further be illustrated with the addition of key variables to the grid:

Interview	Small Group	Public Speech	Theatre/ Concert
Attention Concentration Sensitivity	Attention Concentration Sensitivity	Attention Concentration Sensitivity	Attention Concentration Sensitivity
Attention Concentration Sensory Acuity	Attention Concentration Sensory Acuity	Attention Concentration Sensory Acuity	Attention Concentration Sensory Acuity
Attention Concentration Understanding	Attention Concentration Understanding	Attention Concentration Understanding	Attention Concentration Understanding
Attention Concentration Understanding Empathy	Attention Concentration Understanding Empathy	Attention Concentration Understanding Empathy	Attention Concentration Understanding Empathy
Attention Concentration Understanding Evaluation	Attention Concentration Understanding Evaluation	Attention Concentration Understanding Evaluation	Attention Concentration Understanding Evaluation

Attentive, responsive listening is
essential to whatever role we assume.
Photo by Robert Tocha.

It should be evident, then, that, depending upon the role he or she is to assume and the purpose he or she (as well as the other communicator) wishes to achieve, the listener will set objectives and utilize his or her listening resources. The roles we assume as listeners become, then, important variables in the way we listen and in the responses we give.

Summary

In this chapter, we have looked at the roles a listener assumes. We function informally as listeners in casual conversation; additionally, we assume informal listening roles when we attend to radio and television, most typically alone or with only a few others present, geared as it is to a mass audience. More formally, we function as listeners when we participate in interviews and in group discussions. And we play different roles as members of public audiences (public speeches, theatre, etc.).

The objectives we set for our listening behavior within these roles will depend, to a great extent, upon what we want to get out of the listening experience and upon what the source of the message wants us to get from it. Consequently, attention and concentration are keys to effective listening in all situations, but other factors may vary depending upon our listening goals and the particular demands of the role we must assume.

Activities to Try

1. Listen attentively to a radio broadcast of a radio drama. What efforts are made to communicate the characters and the setting? What efforts were made to create tone and mood? Note vocal work by actors and the sound effects.

2. Watch a television broadcast of a situation comedy taped before a live studio audience. What effect does the audience response have on your responses at home? Do you feel that the presence of audience laughter, applause, etc., causes you to respond at home to situations that you might not find funny if you did not hear the audience response?

3. Arrange to interview a specialist in your major field of study. Ask this person about the role that listening plays in your field. What is the importance of listening in your field? What different types of listening are required at various levels within the field? Ask the specialist to suggest any articles in your field which discuss the role of listening. Draw up a short paper summarizing the role of listening in your field.

4. Arrange to conduct an interview as the interviewer; draw up a schedule to give you some general guidelines as you conduct the questions. Do not take notes, but do arrange to close with a summary of the information you have gained. After the interview, analyze your listening behavior. Were you able to comprehend the interviewee's responses and to adapt your questions to these responses? What were your listening objectives? Did you achieve them? Do you feel that you were an effective listener? Do you feel that the interviewee perceived you as an effective listener? Why or why not?

5. Arrange to participate in a group discussion. In addition to offering meaningful comments, work to be an attentive, comprehensive listener throughout the discussion. As you listen, try to adapt your responses to meet task or maintenance needs of the group as the needs arise. At the end of the discussion, summarize for the group what has been accomplished. After the discussion, analyze your listening behavior. Did you accomplish your objectives as a listener? Were you effective as a listener in the group discussion? Why or why not?

6. Attend a "live" public speech and work to be a comprehensive listener. Observe the other listeners around you. After the speech, try to participate in the question-answer session to clarify any points you may have had difficulty following. Summarize the content of the speech by identifying the central point and the main points of the speech. Was the speech clearly organized? Was it effectively developed and presented? What efforts were made to develop and maintain the group as an audience? Did you note efforts at social facilitation? Polarization? Speaker adaptation to audience feedback? Were you an effective public listener?

7. Attend a "live" theatre production and observe the audience. What efforts were made to develop social facilitation? Polarization? Do you feel that the

actors were responsive to the audience? Was there supportive feedback at the curtain call?

Notes

1. Edmond G. Addeo and Robert E. Burger, *EgoSpeak* (Radnor, Pennsylvania: Chilton Book Company, 1973), p. xii.
2. "Advertisers Keep Spending into the Recession," *Business Week* 2648 (August 4, 1980): 75.
3. Tony Schwartz, "Listen," *T.V. Guide* (February 24, 1979): 5–7.
4. George Gerbner et al., "The 'Mainstreaming' of America: Violence Profile No. 11," *Journal of Communication* 30 (Summer 1980): 13.
5. *Ibid.*, p. 14.
6. Ben Stein, *The View from Sunset Boulevard* (New York: Basic Books, 1979).
7. Louis Harris, "Confidence in Most Institutions Down" ABC News—Harris Survey, 1, 27 (March 5, 1979).
8. "The Miscomprehension of Televised Communications" (Report by the Educational Foundation of the American Association of Advertising Agencies, New York, May 1980), p. 7.
9. Cal W. Downs, Paul Smeyak, and Ernest Martin, *Professional Interviewing* (New York: Harper and Row, 1980), pp. 79–80.
10. S. I. Hayakawa, "How to Attend a Conference" *ETC* 3 (Autumn 1955): 5.
11. Adapted from John Dewey, *How We Think* (Boston: D. C. Heath Company, 1910), pp. 68–78.
12. Ernest G. Bormann and Nancy C. Bormann, *Effective Small Group Communication* (Minneapolis: Burgess Publishing Company, 1976), pp. 27–28.
13. Charles Kelly, "Empathic Listening," in *Small Group Communication: A Reader,* eds. Robert S. Cathcart and Larry A. Samovar (Dubuque, Iowa: William C. Brown Company Publishers, 1970), pp. 257–258.
14. Herbert Kupferberg, "The Audience," *Stagebill* (July 1980), p. 20.
15. H. L. Hollingworth, *The Psychology of the Audience* (New York: American Book Company, 1935), pp. 19–35.
16. Paul D. Holtzman, *The Psychology of Speakers' Audiences* (Glenview, Illinois: Scott, Foresman, 1970), pp. 118–119.

concepts you will encounter

Responsible Decision Making
Self-Concept
Johari Window
Self-Disclosure
Stereotypes
Motivation
Active Listening
Sending Feedback
Caring

responsibilities of the listener 10

While much of what we have described as techniques for listening effectiveness for the various purposes of listening may be construed to be responsibilities for listening behavior for those purposes, there are some responsibilities which are particular to effective listening for all purposes in various settings.

Responsible Listening Decisions

Listening, like much in life, is a matter of responsible decision making. A listener constantly is faced with choices to make about listening. We have defined listening as the process of receiving, attending to, and assigning meaning to aural stimuli. Going back to the Wolvin-Coakley listening model in chapter 3, we can see that the listener must make decisions to, first of all, receive the stimulus. It is possible to decide to hear or not to hear the sound, for example, just by the simple control of the on-off knob on the radio.

The listener must decide, then, to attend to the stimulus. Once you have received it, you can choose to deal with the stimulus or merely to tune it out or avoid it. You might hear an announcement in a shopping mall, for instance, about a store special on omelet pans, but you may select not to attend further to the announcement. Likewise, you make choices about assigning meaning to the stimulus. Do you choose, as an example, to interpret someone's vocal inflections as supportive or as sarcastic in a conversation?

How we handle these choices depends very much on the decisions we make. A listener must decide
    not to listen
    to listen actively
    to listen for appreciation
    to listen for discrimination
    to listen for comprehension
    to listen to provide a therapeutic "sounding board" with empathy
    to listen for critical evaluation
    to set aside biases and attitudes in order to understand the message
    to concentrate on the message, not the speaker
    to overcome emotional barriers in listening
    to know why the listener is listening at a particular time

to know how the listener is listening in the process

to understand the process of listening in order to know what the listener is doing

It may interest you to note that we have included as one choice to decide not to listen. A listener has a responsibility to him- or herself and to the other person to make this choice if it is appropriate. You may choose not to listen, for example, if you do not have the time to listen. If you are having a pressing deadline for a project at work, it would be appropriate to attend to the project and not break your concentration to try to listen to another person. It would be likely that the listening in such a situation would not be particularly satisfying for either party. You would feel frustrated because you need to get on with the project, and the other person would feel frustrated because you are not truly "tuned in" as a listener.

You may need to decide not to listen, also, if you are suffering from what might be termed "information overload." There are times when we all receive too much information at one time, so that it becomes difficult to process it meaningfully. Information overload must be much like the experience of a young child at a theme park—the child cannot possibly take in all the stimuli at one time. Indeed, this example might be descriptive of us as adults as well.

The decision-making process is not easy. The lifetime of experiences, attitudes, knowledge, and skills that make up our frame of reference—our very self—influences the way we deal with these choices. How we react to situations and process them through our own perceptions is a dominant force in our decision making. A listener might decide to listen with careful comprehension, for example, if he or she perceived the outcome to be rewarding. Listening to thoroughly comprehend a lecture in order to do well on a test over the material may be a familiar choice to most of us.

Many decisions we make as listeners relate to others as well as to ourselves. We might listen with empathy to someone we would like to have as a friend, but we might listen more comprehensively if the other person is a stranger who wants to discuss a faulty product. Each listener must make choices based on the relationship he or she has, or wants to have, or does not want to have with the other person.

Whether the decisions affect the listener, the other person, or both, every listening choice creates its own problems, generates its own difficulties, and pays its own rewards. As human beings, listeners make their choices and then must live with the positive or negative consequences of those decisions. It would seem, then, that the responsible listener must be aware of the choices he or she faces, make those choices within some sort of valid framework for him- or herself and the other person, and then be prepared to live with or to change the results of the choices he or she makes. As listeners, then, we have responsibilities both to ourselves and to others.

Responsibilities to Yourself

Understanding the Self

Our first responsibility as effective listeners is to understand ourselves as communicators. Just as the sources of the communication messages should be trained in self-intrapersonal-communication, so, too, should listeners know themselves. Brooks states the case eloquently:

> To see one's self accurately; to understand and know one's self clearly and honestly; to have acquired those abilities and characteristics associated with a strong, wholesome, self-concept—these objectives are directly related to liking one's self, being confident in one's self, and in relating and living effectively and satisfyingly with others.[1]

Learning about yourself has become a major focus of the popular self-help books and workshops (Werner's est, Dyer's *Your Erroneous Zones,* etc.). A useful technique for beginning this self-analysis is through the Johari Window.[2]

The Johari Window (fig. 10.1) accounts for the dimensions of the self. As the diagram indicates, there are four basic areas of the self: free, blind, hidden, and unknown. Area 1 is the open, public self. Area III, the hidden area, could be systematically diminished through communicating information about yourself to others—a process of self-disclosure.

The blind area consists of all information that other persons know about you but that you do not know about yourself. This may be information which individuals are reluctant to reveal to you. Some enterprising individuals have formed companies in metropolitan areas to handle the communication of such messages. One firm in Washington, D.C., for instance, will send a message to your boss that he has bad breath—for a fee of $5.00!

The unknown area represents all aspects of a person which truly are not known to the individual or to others. While some persons might argue that the more you communicate about yourself and create an "open" window, the more you diminish your unknown area, others might suggest we can never specify the unknown and, thus, never narrow our unknown area.

Through self-disclosure, a communicator can design his or her own window so that the configurations may change. Each individual's window, of course, will take different proportions. An open individual might have a window which resembles that in figure 10.2.

The value of self-disclosure for improved mental health has been documented by the pioneer of this technique, Sidney Jourard, who said

> . . . no man can come to know himself except as an outcome of disclosing himself to another person. . . . When a person has been able to disclose himself utterly to another person, he learns how to increase his contact with his real self, and he may then be better able to direct his destiny on the basis of knowledge of his real self.[3]

An understanding of yourself can be of value to you as a listener in knowing something about your self-concept and how it affects your listening behavior.

Figure 10.1.
The Johari Window.
From *Of Human Interaction* by Joseph Luft by permission of Mayfield Publishing Company. Copyright © 1969 by the National Press.

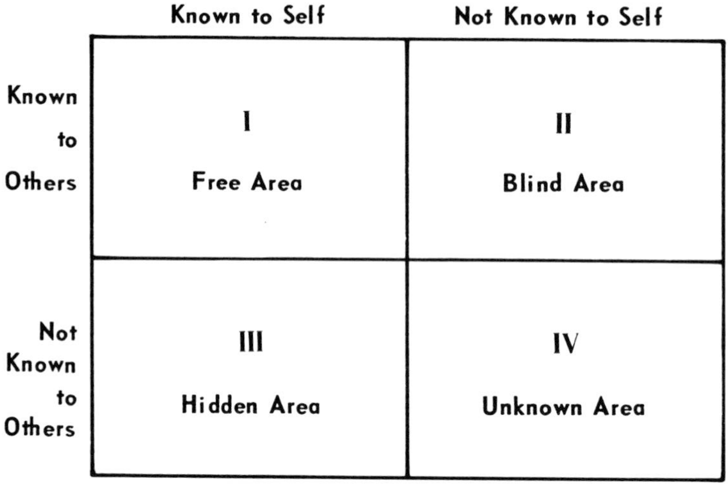
Known to Self
Not Known to Self
Known to Others
Not Known to Others
I
Free Area
II
Blind Area
III
Hidden Area
IV
Unknown Area

Figure 10.2.
The Johari Window as modified through self-disclosure.
From *Of Human Interaction* by Joseph Luft by permission of Mayfield Publishing Company. Copyright © 1969 by the National Press.

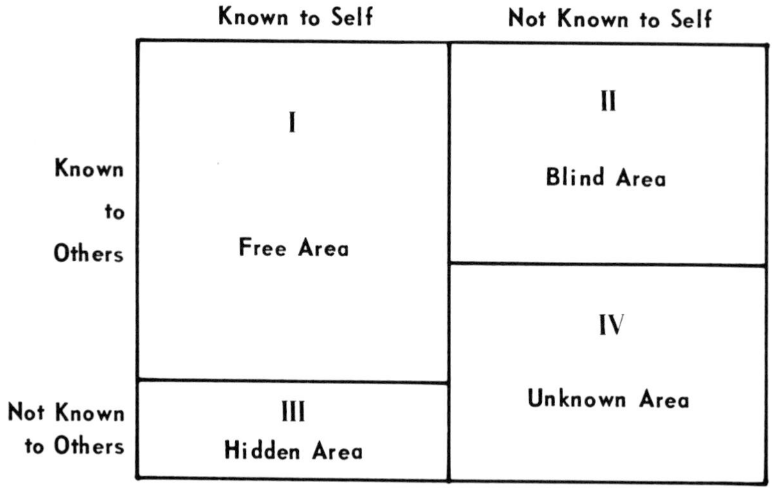
Known to Self
Not Known to Self
Known to Others
Not Known to Others
I
Free Area
II
Blind Area
III
Hidden Area
IV
Unknown Area

The effect of the self-concept on listening behavior has not been researched to any great extent. Research in reading, however, does support the idea that improved self-concepts can improve reception: "Sufficient evidence has been found . . . and enough support from authorities in education and psychology has been accumulated to suggest that many disabled readers can be helped by improving their self-concepts."[4]

For most of us, our listening self-concept is too negative. Throughout our lives, we have probably experienced few rewards for good listening. Instead, we have been subjected to negative reinforcement: "You're not listening to me." "Sit down and listen to me." "You don't listen." "Why don't you ever listen to me?"

Such messages must have a significant impact on the ability to function as a listener. If you are told often enough that you are not a good listener, you will start to believe that you are a poor listener and will behave accordingly. Research in psychology supports the idea that an individual will behave in consistency with his or her self-concept and "live up to the label" through the self-fulfilling prophecy.[5]

Understanding your self-concept also can lead to a better self-understanding of your attitudes not only toward messages you receive but also toward the receiving process itself. Just as a negative attitude may be fostered about our listening behavior, we may come to have a distorted attitude about the process as a passive act. As our model of listening process would indicate, listening is a very active, dynamic act. Through social conditioning at home and at school, however, it is possible that listeners have come to view the listening process as a very passive phenomenon: sit back and let the teacher talk.

Likewise, understanding such attitudes as they may affect listening behavior extends to understanding your own value system. How you process the information you receive through the category system depends, to a great extent, upon how your categories are consistent with what you value. Thus, as a receiver, you run the risk of stereotyping verbal and nonverbal messages and drawing false conclusions from these.[6] Walter Lippmann once explained the concept of stereotypes as representing

> . . . an ordered, more or less consistent picture of the world, to which our habits, our tastes, our capacities, our comforts, and our hopes have adjusted themselves. They may not be a complete picture of the world, but they are a picture of a possible world to which we are adapted. In that world people and things have their well-known places, and do certain expected things. We feel at home there. . . .[7]

Understanding our own listening behavior, then, involves discovering our self-concept, attitudes, and values as they relate to our listening responses. We owe it to ourselves to know how we are responding and to sincerely attempt to overcome any of the pitfalls in the process.

Motivating the Listening Self

As a second listening responsibility to ourselves, we should strive for individual motivation in the process. As we have defined listening as an active process, involving complex interaction of our sensory channels, the responsible listeners should recognize that they cannot remain passive partners in the communication.

Carl Weaver notes that developing a desire to listen is basic to effective listening. Unfortunately, developing this desire is not a simple behavioral act, for, as Weaver notes, "most people do not really want to listen, but to talk."[8] He recommends that the desire to listen requires that the listener suppress the desire to talk and develop a desire to learn. We have a capacity to listen, composed of all those dimensions treated in this book, but this capactiy to listen is not meaningful unless we combine it with a willingness to listen.[9]

The impact of motivation on listening comprehension was demonstrated in a recent study in which subjects were asked to comprehend and recall information presented via compressed speech tapes. Subjects in one of the groups were promised extra credit points commensurate with their comprehension scores as an added incentive to performing well as listeners. The results of this experiment suggest that the motivated group did score higher, leading researchers to conclude that the capacity to listen coupled with the willingness to listen does affect listening performance.[10]

Since listening requires active behaviors, good listeners will assume the responsibility for their own motivation to listen and not passively wait for the speaker to provide such motivation. Indeed, this overreliance on the speaker to carry the burden in the communication process results in serious barriers to effective communication transactions. Further, such passive behavior on the part of most of us as listeners almost represents a cultural conditioning: we have come to expect to rely on the speaker for motivation. The speaker who fails to provide such motivation too frequently is tuned out. Such an attitude toward the motivation to listen is irresponsible because it represents an abrogation of the equal responsibility to make a communication work.

Building intrinsic motivation to listen is not easy. There is no specific drive to listen. A combination of factors enters into our motivation—drives, habits, predispositions, cognitive states. If the listening experience can fulfill basic needs, then the motivation can be maintained at a high level. The maintenance can be assisted by efforts on the part of the listener to establish goals and identify specific purposes for listening before entering the listening setting.

Likewise, the listener can enhance his or her intrinsic motivation to listen by establishing his or her own reward system.[11] Rather than relying on external rewards (gold stars from teachers, etc.), we can motivate ourselves by providing our own satisfactions for effective listening. Often this reward system can result from establishing and then accomplishing the goal in the listening situation. For instance, you might set as your goal the acquisition of new information from a technical briefing in a field with which you are not familiar. Your internal reward can stem from the satisfaction of knowing that you did listen well and that you did gain new information.

We ought to consider the effect of social conditioning on our listening motivation as well. We tend to emphasize the passive nature of listening in American society. School children are expected to "Be quite and listen." And adults are advised to "Just sit back and listen" by emcees, personnel trainers, and even ministers. We should reorient our communication to the advice, "Sit *up* and listen."

To establish internal motivators, obviously, requires the listener to place greater premium on effective listening behavior. It would seem, therefore, that we have a tremendous responsibility to ourselves to place a higher priority on listening motivation.

Responsibilities to Others

Active Listening
In addition to having responsibilities to ourselves as listeners, we have responsibilities to listen actively to others. Since communication is a two-way process, it is important that listeners assume fifty percent of the burden in communicating. While it may seem simplistic to advise one to listen, it is unfortunate that many people do not assume the responsibility of active listening. We are too anxious to let the speaker carry the burden of communication; we too frequently dismiss poor listening with "Oh, he's a boring speaker" or "What a worthless subject."

Our willingness to actively listen throughout the communication should be recognized as a parallel to our right to free speech. Just as speakers have the right to speak out in our society, so, too, do listeners have the right to listen with responsibility. Thus, we need to be willing to meet this obligation and listen to the entire message before passing judgment. Don Oberdorfer described the problem of hecklers in the 1972 presidential campaign:

> Flanked by prominent state legislators and other Wisconsin politicians in their square-cut business suits, Senator Edmund Muskie stood in the ballroom of the Loraine Hotel (in Madison) and faced this dissonant music.
>
> "I came here this afternoon—"
>
> "To get votes" gleefully shouted a girl in the back of the hall.
>
> The students laughed, and a blond young man in front, smirking broadly, chimed in, "Is everybody happy?"
>
> "Let the man rap," yelled an older student with a beard and dark glasses, and a portion of the crowd agreed.
>
> "My purpose in coming to Madison this afternoon . . ." the candidate began again, only to be interrupted by shouts and insults, some of them obscene. He was told what he was full of, and a young brown-shirted boy weaved up through the crowd and waved a marijuana cigarette in his face. Muskie said, "No thanks," and stared him down. The grinning cigarette waver finally returned to his seat on the floor.
>
> After nearly an hour of this, the presidential candidate uttered an ironic thanks and went away to the next stop on his campaign trail.[12]

Sending Feedback

People who share the responsibility as communicators and allow the speakers the chance to present their messages serve as active listeners throughout listening situations. And this responsibility extends beyond the listening process to sending open, honest, constructive, meaningful feedback.

Barker offers ten basic guidelines for sending feedback effectively:

1. Send feedback that is appropriate to the speaker's message.
2. Be certain the speaker perceived the feedback.
3. Make certain the feedback is clear in meaning.
4. Send the feedback quickly.
5. Beware of overloading the system.
6. Delay in performing any activity that might create an unintentional effect.
7. Keep feedback to the message separate from personal evaluation.
8. Use nondirective feedback until the speaker invites evaluation of his message.
9. Be certain that you understand the message before you send directive feedback.
10. Realize that early attempts at giving more effective feedback may seem unnatural but will improve with practice.[13]

As general guidelines for sending feedback, Barker's suggestions can prove to be useful. Listeners need to sharpen their feedback skills and recognize that they are sending verbal and nonverbal messages through the feedback channel. Since sending feedback is a continuous process while we are communicating with someone, it is important that the feedback be expressive of what it is we want to communicate to the other person.

A good listener will avoid sending distracting, unintentional feedback through responses that may not be appropriate to the situation. And a good listener will recognize that open, honest feedback certainly is the best form of communication. We recognize, however, that honest feedback may sometimes have a negative effect on a speaker and lead to the ending of the communication. Consequently, the listener should assess carefully the possible effects of his or her response and judge accordingly.

Barker's point that concentration on feedback skills, like many of the listening skills we have described, may seem unnatural at first is well-taken. Listeners can find, however, that, once they have used the feedback skills for a time, they will begin to feel comfortable with these skills.

Through these guidelines, you can improve your own feedback and, thus, enhance the process within your own communication worlds. As responsible listeners, we ought to pay more attention to being effective sources of feedback messages. Meaningful feedback is vital to a meaningful communication interaction with others. The rewards to both speaker and listener can be extensive.

These four responsibilities—to know yourself, to motivate yourself, to listen actively, and to send appropriate feedback—can help us to function as more effective and more meaningful communicators. Self-awareness is the first step toward improving listening behavior. The next step, of course, is to rigorously

By accepting the responsibility of genuinely *caring* about how our listening behavior affects us as well as others, we become "people hearing *with* listening."
Photo by Robert Tocha.

apply principles of effective listening to your own listening behavior in all your communication situations. Dominick Barbara best summed up this next step:

> To discover order and honesty in his perceiving, Man must have the courage to face the truth within himself. His listening must remain free of prejudiced distortions, false condemnations, and personal resentments. Furthermore, he must be honest enough to develop a realistic understanding of his own motives and the actions to which he is driven by them. The more able he is to listen on a rational, responsible and humanistic basis, the more readily will Man ultimately realize himself and discover his most constructive possibilities.[14]

This realization of our abilities as total communicators can help us to overcome our failure to listen and, hopefully, enable us to begin to achieve greater social priority for effective listening. Perhaps then we can be a nation of "people hearing *with* listening. . . ."

Listen to Care

Each semester, as a project in our listening course, we ask our students to interview a person whose livelihood depends to a great extent on effective listening. Students interview a variety of professionals—psychiatrists, counselors, physicians, attorneys, customer service representatives, ministers, diplomats, account clerks. The interviews yield interesting information about how these listeners do listen and what techniques and training they feel are important. Much of the information parallels what we have covered in this book, but there is a further dimension to effective listening which professional listeners almost always cite— *care*. They stress that all the techniques and theory prove to be meaningless unless listeners assume responsibility for the process by genuinely caring about how their listening behavior will affect them as well as the others in the communication.

Taking the time and the trouble to listen well is rewarding. If you care about yourself as a listener and if you care about the other person as a human being, you both will feel enriched for the experience. And that intangible reward may be the greatest payoff we have in human relationships at home, at work, and in the world at large.

Summary

In this chapter, we have stressed the importance of effective listeners to fulfill certain basic responsibilities to themselves as listeners and to other communicators. The responsible listener, then, should understand him- or herself as a communicator and should strive for self-motivation as a listener. Both responsibilities require considerable self-analysis and applications to listening behavior.

In addition, the responsible listener has obligations to other communicators to listen actively in order to participate as an equal partner in the communication process. And the responsible listener works at sending open, honest, constructive, meaningful feedback so as to enhance the communication process and to enable the speaker to adapt his or her message as necessary.

Since we have the right to free speech in the United States, with its accompanying obligation to impart responsible messages, it stands to reason that we should take seriously, also, our right to "free listening" and the obligation that, likewise, assumes.

Activities to Try

1. Interview two people who are especially effective as listeners (perhaps professional counselors or friends/family members who are "noted" for listening). Ask them to reflect on their techniques and on their sense of responsibility to themselves and to other communicators.
2. Interview a politician who has recently conducted an election/re-election campaign. Ask the person about the general responsiveness of his or her audiences and his or her impression of how seriously his or her listeners had taken their responsibilities as listeners. What do you perceive to be the general state of listening responsibility in the United States?

3. Participate in a self-disclosure conversation with another person on some topics that you have not discussed before. After the discussion, draw your Johari Window and discuss it with your partner. Does it reflect the extent to which you did self-disclose? What did you learn, then, about your self-concept through the Window?

4. Create a list or a chart of those ideas and beliefs which are important (of value) to you. Then, do another list or chart of those things which you value. What do these lists or charts tell you about yourself? What do they tell you, then, about your listening behavior? Do these values influence the perceptions through which you listen? How?

5. Practice the skill of sending feedback to speakers in interviews, group discussions, and public speeches. Make a conscious effort to apply the principles enumerated by Barker (as detailed in this chapter). Ask the speakers to whom you send feedback what their impressions are. Does your feedback communicate the messages you intend? Are you effective at sending feedback?

Notes

1. William D. Brooks, *Speech Communication,* 3rd ed. (Dubuque, Iowa: Wm. C. Brown Company Publishers, 1978), p. 56.
2. Joseph Luft, *Group Process: An Introduction to Group Dynamics* (Palo Alto, California: National Press, 1963).
3. Sidney M. Jourard, *The Transparent Self* (New York: Van Nostrand Reinhold Company, 1964), p. 5.
4. Ivan Quandt, *Self-Concept and Reading* (Newark, Delaware: International Reading Association, no date), p. 31.
5. For an interesting review of some of the research on the self-fulfilling prophecy, see Robert Rosenthal, "Self-Fulfilling Prophecy," *Readings in Psychology Today* (Del Mar, California: CRM Books, 1967), pp. 466–471.
6. For a dated but interesting review of research on stereotyping, see William L. Brembeck and William S. Howell, *Persuasion* (Englewood Cliffs, New Jersey: Prentice-Hall, Inc., 1952), pp. 108–119.
7. Walter Lippmann, *Public Opinion* (New York: The Macmillan Company, 1922), p. 95.
8. Carl Weaver, *Human Listening: Process and Behavior* (Indianapolis: Bobbs-Merrill, 1972), p. 82.
9. Weaver notes this distinction and emphasizes the importance of the willingness to listen, *Ibid.,* pp. 7–8.
10. Michael J. Beatty, Ralph R. Behnke, and Deidre L. Froelich, "Effects of Achievement Incentive and Presentation Rate on Listening Comprehension," *The Quarterly Journal of Speech* 66 (April 1980): 193–200.

11. Motivation researchers have come to regard motivation as equivalent to reinforcement. See, for example, Robert C. Bolles, *Theory of Motivation* (New York: Harper and Row Publishers, 1967), ch. 15.
12. Don Oberdorfer, "The Hecklers Return," *The Washington Post* (Sunday 6 February, 1972), p. B7. Reprinted by permission.
13. Larry L. Barker, *Listening Behavior* (Englewood Cliffs, New Jersey: Prentice-Hall, Inc., 1971), pp. 123–124.
14. Dominick A. Barbara, *The Art of Listening* (Springfield, Illinois: Charles C. Thomas Publisher, 1958), p. 191.

bibliography

Barbara, Dominick. *The Art of Listening.* Springfield, Illinois: Charles C. Thomas, 1968.

Barker, Larry L. *Listening Behavior.* Englewood Cliffs, New Jersey: Prentice-Hall, 1971.

Brown, Roger. *Words and Things.* New York: Free Press of Glencoe, 1958.

Colburn, C. William, and Weinberg, Sanford B. *An Orientation to Listening and Audience Analysis.* Chicago: Science Research Associates, 1976.

Duker, Sam. *Listening: Readings.* New York: The Scarecrow Press, 1966.

————. *Listening Bibliography.* Metuchen, New Jersey: The Scarecrow Press, 1968.

————. *Listening: Readings II.* Metuchen, New Jersey: The Scarecrow Press, 1971.

Friedman, Paul G. *Listening Processes: Attention, Understanding, Evaluation.* Washington, D.C.: National Education Association, 1978.

Geeting, Baxter, and Geeting, Corinne. *How To Listen Assertively.* New York: Monarch Press, 1976.

Gigous, Goldie M. *Improving Listening Skills.* Dansville, New York: Owen Publishing Corporation, 1967.

Girzaius, Loretta. *Listening a Response Ability.* Winona, Minnesota: St. Mary's College Press, 1972.

Hirsch, Robert O. *Listening: A Way to Process Information Aurally.* Dubuque, Iowa: Gorsuch Scarisbrick, Publishers, 1979.

Johnson, Wendell. *Your Most Enchanted Listener.* New York: Harper & Row, 1956.

Keefe, William F. *Listen, Management!* New York: McGraw-Hill Book Company, 1971.

Long, Lynette. *Listening/Responding.* Monterey, California: Brooks/Cole Publishing Company, 1978.

Lundsteen, Sara W. *Listening: Its Impact on Reading and the Other Language Arts.* Urbana, Illinois: ERIC Clearinghouse on the Teaching of English, 1971.

Mills, Ernest Parker. *Listening: Key to Communication.* New York: Petrocelli Books, 1974.

Moray, Neville. *Listening and Attention.* Baltimore: Penguin Books, 1969.

Nichols, Ralph G., and Stevens, Leonard A. *Are You Listening?* New York: McGraw-Hill Book Company, 1957.

Schwartz, Tony. *The Responsive Chord.* New York: Anchor Books, 1974.

Taylor, Stanford E. *Listening.* Washington, D.C.: National Education Association, 1973.

Weaver, Carl H. *Human Listening: Processes and Behavior.* Indianapolis: Bobbs-Merrill Company, 1972.

Wolvin, Andrew D., and Coakley, Carolyn Gwynn. *Listening Instruction.* Urbana, Illinois: ERIC Clearinghouse on Reading and Communication Skills, 1979.

index

Borman, Nancy C., 157, 164
Bormann, Ernest G., 157, 164
Bostrom, Robert N., viii
Bower, Gordon H., 57
Brammer, Lawrence M., 115, 122
Brembeck, William, L., 177
Brieter, Lila R., 4, 14
Brigance, William N., 82
Broadbent, D. E., 41, 57
Brooks, William D., 169, 177
Brown, Charles T., 9, 15, 104
Brown, Donald P., 9, 16, 32, 56
Brown, James I., 30, 56, 97, 98, 103, 104, 105
Brown, Kenneth L., 10–11, 16
Brown, Roger, 45, 58
Brown-Carlsen Listening Comprehension Test, 56, 97, 103, 104
Bruner, Jerome S., 45, 58
Bryant, Carol L., viii
Buktenica, Norman A., 83
Burger, Robert E., 151, 164
Business Week, 152

Caffrey, John, 29, 32, 55, 56, 103
Calero, Henry H., 80, 83
Caring, 175–176
Carlsen, G. Robert, 30, 56, 97, 98, 103, 104, 105
Carter, Jimmy, 129
Cathcart, Robert S., 122, 164
Chapin, Richard E., 15
Chase, William G., 86, 103
CIBA Pharmaceutical, 36
Clearinghouse on Reading and Communication Skills, 33
Clearinghouse on the Teaching of English, 33
Clevenger, Theodore, Jr., 128, 147
Coakley, Carolyn Gwynn, 16, 34, 106
Coercion, 126
Coger, Leslie Irene, 65, 70
Cohen, Alexander, 57
Colburn, C. William, 142, 148
Cole, Ronald A., 82
Commission on the English Curriculum of the National Council of Teachers of English, 6, 7, 15, 50, 58
Communication
apprehension, 21

as a simultaneous process, 23–25
components of, 19–20
channel, 19
environment, 19–20
feedback, 19
message, 19
noise, 20
external, 20
internal, 20
receiver, 19
source, 19
context, 161–162
interactional, 19, 24
levels, 5–8
group, 5
interpersonal, 5, 8
mass, 5–8
public, 5
process of, 19–26
symbolic, 23
transactional, 23–25
two-step flow of, 7–8
variables, 20–23
attitudes, 21
knowledge, 20–21
language code, 22
message, 22
skills, 20
Comprehensive listening, 84–102
skills, 88–100
uses of, 85
variables, 85–88
Compressed speech, 88–90
speech compressors, 90
AmBiChron Model 101, 90
Varispeed-II, 90
VSC Speech Controller, 90
uses of, 89–90
Concentration, 85, 86, 98
Condon, Edwyna F., 103
Conversation, 151–152, 160–161
and listening effectiveness, 151–152
and nonlistening, 151
Correlation coefficient, 87, 104
Cosgrove, Michael, 99
Cowan, J. L., 82
Critical Listening, 124–146
and listeners' responsibilities, 145
need for, 125–127
and the process of persuasion, 126–127